THE CHINA EMPLOYMENT LAW GUIDE

THE CHINA EMPLOYMENT LAW GUIDE

What You Need to Know to Protect Your Company

FIRST EDITION

GRACE YANG

ISBN: 978-1-63161-041-7

Published by TCK Publishing

www.TCKPublishing.com

Get discounts and special deals on our best selling books at

www.tckpublishing.com/bookdeals

CONTENTS

INTRODUCTION

Where I excel is ridiculous, sickening, work ethic.
You know, while the other guy's sleeping? I'm working.

~ Will Smith

All things are difficult before they are easy
(万事开头难).

~ Chinese proverb

Doing business in China can be a tremendously profitable, thrilling experience. Whether you're building a manufacturing business from scratch, expanding your software company into Asian markets, or partnering with local executives on the ground to bring a brilliant idea for a medical supply business to life, you're geared for adventure.

To ignite that vision, however, you need to understand and address technical labor issues. How should you hire local workers? What contracts do you need, and what language needs to be included in them and why? What processes and procedures must you put in place to respect local and national laws, to minimize surprises, to avoid hassles and interference from the government, and to resolve disputes in a mindful, strategic way?

The hyper-local nature of Chinese employment law — along with the fact that this law is constantly evolving — creates a profound set of challenges. After all, the key to growing any enterprise is clarity. You need to minimize your blind spots. That's hard to do in any environment, but it's especially tough when you're setting up shop in a foreign country whose character, labor markets, and legal frameworks are as complex as China's.

So what should you do? How can you build up your business in China and achieve your dream outcome?

The *China Employment Law Guide* offers an essential reference.

This book consists of hand-selected blog posts and articles my colleagues and I have authored over the years at our very popular China Law Blog,[1] which the American Bar Association recently lauded as one of the Top 20 law blogs on the entire internet.[2] (We are constantly updating this blog, so please bookmark it to get our latest thoughts and insights!)

This guide is not meant to be consumed in one sitting.

Rather, we compiled these articles to serve as a timely and (we hope) entertaining manual to reference as various problems surface for your business, your managers, and your H.R. department.

Please review the Table of Contents (located just before this introduction) and jump ahead to read about whatever issue seems most urgent to you and your company.

We've divided the book into three sections. The first is all about **China Labor Contracts**. In this section we discuss: the basics of hiring employees; critical rules for handling employment contracts; the Double-Wage Penalty; hiring foreign workers in China; and many other fascinating and useful topics.

The next section covers the inevitable **Bumps in the Road** that you and your company will encounter managing your team. Topics include: China's surprising laws regarding mass layoffs; the challenges of lifetime employees and what to do about them; the dangers of

---

[1]   http://www.chinalawblog.com

[2]   http://www.abajournal.com/magazine/article/2013_blawg_100_hall_of_fame

employment offer letters; and what happens when WFOEs run out of money to continue doing business in China.

Finally, we'll dive into some **Frequently Asked Questions about China Employment Law**. We'll cover how vacation law works in China; how student interns need to be treated; the complicated employment laws on the treatment of pregnant and nursing employees; and much more.

This book is not a do-it-yourself "how to" guide to China employment law, nor should it be substituted for the counsel of a qualified China employment law attorney. We hope, however, that it answers some of the key questions you and your team have, and that it gives you the peace of mind you need to compete.

If you need help with a China employment law issue, call Harris Bricken at 206-224-5657 to schedule a consultation with Grace Yang,[3] or learn more at http://www.harrisbricken.com.[4]

---

[3] http://harrisbricken.com/our-team/grace-yang
[4] http://www.harrisbricken.com/

SECTION ONE

CHINA LABOR CONTRACTS

It takes ten years to grow trees but a hundred years to rear people
(十年树木, 百年树人).

~ Chinese proverb

CHINA EMPLOYMENT LAW: THE BASICS ON NEW HIRES

If you plan to hire new employees in China, there are a number of employment law issues you should consider. Let's briefly discuss a few of these issues.

If your new hire had a previous job in China, you should require your new hire to provide proof (usually consisting of a document from his or her previous employer) that the previous employment relationship ended properly. This is not a legal requirement, but will serve your interests. You want your employee to be dedicated to working for just you, so you want to make sure he or she will not continue working for some other employer. You would be surprised (or maybe you wouldn't) at how often someone seeks to secretly hold two jobs in China, especially for two different WFOEs. To that end, you will also want to make clear in your offer letters, contracts, and in your rules and regulations[5] that holding more than one job is prohibited. We see it all the time in China: an employee believes he or she is underpaid so they get a second job or start their own side business in competition with yours. Although you may not care if your employee is selling Gucci bags on WeChat, you will want to make sure your employee's moonlighting does not adversely affect the employee's work

---

[5] http://www.chinalawblog.com/2016/04/china-employer-rules-and-regulations-and-why-you-must-have-one.html

performance or your company. You want to make it easy to terminate[6] an employee whose extracurricular activities are harming your business.

Before you bring on any new China-based employee, you should also make sure there are no unresolved issues between your new hire and his or her previous employer. One issue that often comes up is the non-compete agreement.[7] If you did not ask your new hire if he or she ever signed a non-compete with the previous employer, you may be at risk. Even if the new hire is a relatively low-level employee,[8] it is still possible that the employee signed a non-compete. If you are considered a competitor under that non-compete, hiring that person could subject you to liability. Get your potential hire to provide you with a copy of any non-compete agreement *and* a copy of his or her current or previous labor contract. Chinese courts have upheld the validity of one-sentence non-compete provisions in labor contracts.

You also should confirm whether your new hire in China has completed the hand-over and exit procedures of his or her previous employer. Many China employers require their employees to cooperate during the exit process and a failure to do so could subject the employee to liability. We find it very helpful to learn how new hires handled these exit procedures because how they did so can tell you a lot about them.

It also makes sense to try to determine whether your potential new employee gave adequate notice of leaving to his or her previous employer. If he or she did not, the previous employer can sue your new hire for damages, which is not something you want new employees to be bogged down with during their first few months with your company. And how they treated their previous employer will be a good indication of how they will treat you.

Once your new hire officially starts working for you under a written labor contract,[9] you can now sit back and relax and revel in your

---

[6] http://www.chinalawblog.com/2010/01/terminating_your_china_employe.html
[7] http://www.chinalawblog.com/2014/09/china-non-competes-oh-oh-the-price-youll-pay.html
[8] http://www.chinalawblog.com/2016/02/china-non-competes.html
[9] http://www.chinalawblog.com/2015/07/dont-get-lazy-with-your-china-employment-contracts.html

ability to recruit great new talent, right? Not exactly. Under China employment law, your new hire can leave by giving you three days' notice. And this notice need not be in writing. Don't bother trying to enlarge this notice requirement — you cannot make it any longer than what the law requires.

Do not forget to have your new hire's social insurance and employee files properly transferred and set up in a timely manner. The probation period is considered part of the employment period, and just because an employee will not complete his or her probation period for six months does not mean you can wait that long to pay his or her social insurance.

Finally, keep in mind that if an "employee" has been working for you as a dispatched worker, he or she should not be considered a new hire for purposes of China's labor laws. Therefore, you may not set an additional probation period for this employee when he or she becomes your direct hire.

EIGHT BASIC RULES FOR YOUR CHINA EMPLOYMENT CONTRACTS

1. **Use a written employment contract.**[10]
   The employer penalties for not doing so can be (and usually are) huge. This one is a no-brainer. Oh, and China pretty much does not have independent contractors. See China's Tax Authorities Want You.[11]

2. **Use a China-centric employment contract.**[12]
   Your employment contracts should be written for China. Though it occasionally makes sense for large multinationals that want all of their employment contracts worldwide to be similar, a China-specific employment contract will be better.

3. **Use an employee rules and regulations manual.**[13]
   These are not optional for China. Maintaining detailed employee

---

[10] http://www.chinalawblog.com/2015/05/china-employment-contracts-if-yours-are-not-current-you-have-a-problem.html

[11] http://www.forbes.com/sites/danharris/2015/05/28/chinas-tax-authorities-want-you/

[12] http://www.chinalawblog.com/2014/10/china-employment-contracts-do-not-try-this-at-home-part-ii.html

[13] http://www.chinalawblog.com/2011/09/china_employee_contracts_and_employee_manuals.html

rules and regulations is especially important for terminating an employee beyond his or her probationary period. In disputes over whether an employee has been wrongfully terminated, the burden is on the employer to clearly prove cause for termination. If the employer cannot show clear discipline records to establish grounds for the dismissal, the employer will likely lose.

4. **Use probationary periods.**[14]
   China is not an at-will employment jurisdiction; you need a good reason to fire someone. But China typically allows a probationary period where termination is considerably easier.

5. **Use your employment contract to nail down your IP.**
   If appropriate (and often it is not), you should use your China employment contracts to address trade secrets,[15] IP ownership,[16] and competition by your employees.[17]

6. **Use the right entity.**
   Make sure your employment contract lists the correct company as the employer. Too often we see employment contracts that were written before our client formed their China WFOE and then never changed after the WFOE was formed. For various reasons, you do not want this.

7. **Use the right law and the right language.**
   For employees in China, China law applies. Some Chinese judges will not recognize employment agreements in any language other than Chinese. So, put your China employment contracts in Chinese.[18] Many employment rules vary by the province and even by city. It is therefore critical that your employment contracts, your rules and regulations, and your employment-related actions all be done pursuant to *local* requirements.

---

[14] http://www.chinalawblog.com/2014/03/china-employment-contracts-the-basics-on-probation.html

[15] http://www.chinalawblog.com/2013/01/the-five-keys-to-china-trade-secret-protection.html

[16] http://www.chinalawblog.com/2012/10/how-to-protect-your-ip-from-china-part-5.html

[17] http://www.chinalawblog.com/2015/08/china-employee-non-compete-agreements-whats-your-geographic-scope.html

[18] http://www.chinalawblog.com/2014/12/china-employment-contracts-why-ours-are-in-chinese.html

8. **Make sure your employees renew their employment contracts before their old ones expire.**[19]
   If you don't complete this step, you may be penalized for not having a written contract with your employees.

---

[19] http://www.chinalawblog.com/2015/07/dont-get-lazy-with-your-china-employment-contracts.html

TEN MORE THINGS TO CONSIDER

Here are the top ten things you should consider when employing anyone in China.

1. **Term of employment.**

    China's employment system is a contract employment system.[20] This means each employee must be hired pursuant to a written contract. This also means it is very difficult to fire an employee during the term of that contract. After the initial contract term expires, you may re-hire the employee pursuant to a second fixed-term contract. In most places in China, the employee will automatically be converted into an employee with an open contract term at the end of the fixed term. This means you have only one chance to hire an employee on a fixed-term basis, so you should be sure to use an appropriate initial employment term. We usually (but not always) recommend an initial term of three years because that allows you to provide a six-month probation period (the longest period permitted under Chinese law) during which time you can more easily terminate an employee and because it delays the onset of the open-term period long enough to allow you to determine whether it makes sense to convert the employee to an open-term employee.

---

[20] http://www.chinalawblog.com/2016/04/china-employer-rules-and-regulations-and-why-you-must-have-one.html

2.   **Salary.**
      Your written employment contract must set forth a salary. One issue to consider here is whether to pay a 13ᵗʰ month in salary, which is customary in many parts of China, and is typically paid out before the Chinese New Year. This is not required, but if you decide to do it, you will want to specify clearly and in writing the conditions for receiving this 13ᵗʰ month salary or you may have to pay this bonus forever – even though you wanted to preserve your option to do otherwise.

3.   **Bonus.**
      If you are going to have a bonus system for your employees, you should set out its parameters in the employment contracts.

4.   **Vacation.**
      The statutory vacation period is based on years of service, as follows:

      - More than 1 and less than 10 years' service: 5 days' vacation.
      - More than 10 and less than 20 years' service: 10 days' vacation.
      - More than 20 years' service: 15 days' vacation.

      If you want to provide more vacation time than set forth above, you should so specify in the contract.

5.   **Other benefits.**
      Your company's rules and regulations[21] typically provide for the statutory minimum and apply to all employees. If you want to provide additional benefits to a particular employee, you should put that in that employee's employment contract. If you wish to provide other benefits beyond the statutory minimum to all of your employees, it usually makes sense for you to spell that out in your rules and regulations.

6.   **Travel.**
      If your employees will travel domestically or internationally, you should have a written travel expense policy.

---

[21] http://www.chinalawblog.com/2016/04/china-employer-rules-and-regulations-and-why-you-must-have-one.html

7. **Overtime.**

You will generally be required to pay overtime to any employee who works beyond the normal working time of eight hours a day and five days a week. If this standard system does not work for you, you should consider adopting an alternative working-hours system for a given employee. See China's Forty Hour Work Week Is Mandatory. Except When It's Not;[22] China's Forty Hour Work Week Is Mandatory. Except When It's Not. Part II;[23] and China's Forty Hour Work Week Is Mandatory. Except When It's Not. Part III.[24]

8. **Trade Secrets/IP Protection.**

If IP is important to you (and most of the time it most certainly should be), you should have a separate Trade Secrecy and IP protection agreement with your employees.

9. **Rules and Regulations.[25]**

You *must* have them. You will also want to make sure that your employees acknowledge – in writing – that they have received this document and that they agree to abide by it.

10. **It's complicated and it's local.**

I don't mean to scare you here (actually I do), but Chinese employment laws and regulations change often and are often local[26] so your employment contracts should always be in Chinese.[27] If this doesn't scare you, it should.

---

[22] http://www.chinalawblog.com/2014/06/china-2.html

[23] http://www.chinalawblog.com/2014/06/chinas-forty-hour-work-week-is-mandatory-except-when-its-not-part-ii.html

[24] http://www.chinalawblog.com/2014/08/chinas-forty-hour-work-week-is-mandatory-except-when-its-not-part-iii.html

[25] http://www.chinalawblog.com/2016/04/china-employer-rules-and-regulations-and-why-you-must-have-one.html

[26] http://www.chinalawblog.com/2015/12/china-employment-law-local-and-not-so-simple.html

[27] http://www.chinalawblog.com/2014/12/china-employment-contracts-why-ours-are-in-chinese.html

CHINA EMPLOYMENT CONTRACTS AND THE DOUBLE WAGE PENALTY

China's labor laws mandate that China employers must have written employment contracts with each of their full-time employees. If an employer goes more than one month without having a written employment contract with an employee, the employer will be required to pay the employee *double* the employee's monthly wage and immediately execute a written labor contract with the employee.

Essentially, PRC labor laws do not hold the employer on the hook for the first month without a written contract. Instead the clock starts running the second month. For example, an employee who starts work on April 1, 2014 but does not enter into a written employment contract with the employer is not entitled to double wages for the month of April. The employer gets a one month free pass.

But suppose there is still no written employment contract in place come May 1, 2014, and that continues to be the case. In that circumstance, the employer will be liable to the employee for double the employee's monthly wage for every month without a written contract. Is there any limit on how many months an employer must pay double wages for not having a written employment contract with an employee? Most jurisdictions end the double-wage penalty after the first year (that is, 11 months, because the employer gets a "free pass" for the first month). But at that point, the employer will be deemed to have entered into an open-term labor contract with that employee. And because this is about as close as one can get to lifetime employment, this is not a situation any employer wants to create.

How long can an employee wait before pursuing a claim for double wages? The usual statute of limitations for China labor law disputes is one year. When does this one-year clock start ticking? Some jurisdictions in China tend to categorize a double-wage payment as labor compensation, but others categorize it as a penalty for violating the law. If it's the former, then the one year statute of limitations does not begin to run until after the employee ceases his or her employment. If it's the latter, the one year statute of limitations begins to run as soon as the employee knows, or should have known, the injury has occurred.

To make things even more complicated, some China labor arbitrators use a third method to calculate the one year statute of limitations. They calculate from the last day of the employee's first year of employment.

BOTTOM LINE: It cannot be stressed enough that you should use a written employment contract with all your employees AND use an appropriate one. And one more thing: just about anyone in China who is doing work as an individual on behalf of your company is your employee. For more on this, check out China's Tax Authorities Want You.[28]

---

[28] http://www.forbes.com/sites/danharris/2015/05/28/chinas-tax-authorities-want-you/

HIRING FOREIGN EMPLOYEES IN CHINA

H iring a foreigner in China usually requires the at each of the following are true:

- The candidate is in good health and over the age of 18;

- The candidate possesses the skills and work experience required for the job;

- The candidate has no criminal record;

- The candidate has a specific employer; and

- The candidate holds a valid passport or another valid travel document in lieu of a passport.

Note, though, that the local rules need to be consulted and, like everything else regarding China employment law, they can vary by locale.[29] For example, some municipalities require a different number of years of work experience. And there are almost always exceptions to the general rules. For example, even though most places impose an upper limit on the candidate's age, many allow exceptions for candidates that satisfy certain other conditions. In some places many

---

[29] http://www.chinalawblog.com/2015/12/china-employment-law-local-and-not-so-simple.html

(sometimes most or all) of the local rules and exceptions are not available to the public and the only way to know what you as an employer can or cannot do is to hash it out by talking with the relevant authorities. This can add confusion and make it difficult to get things right. Bottom line, if you really want to hire an employee who does not satisfy the requirements listed above, you should absolutely **not** give up.

Employers generally need to follow certain steps to bring on a foreigner as an employee. First, the employer must obtain an employment license from the local labor authorities and then secure a work visa invitation confirmation letter from the relevant foreign affairs office. With that letter, the employee may then apply for a work visa at the Chinese Embassy in the employee's home country. Upon arrival in China, the employee must obtain (1) an alien employment permit from the relevant labor authorities, and (2) an alien residence permit from the relevant public security department. Note that these permits need to be updated periodically.

A company that employs a foreigner must do so via a written employment contract that complies with applicable national, provincial, and local laws and regulations. For example, most places require that the contract term for a foreign employee not exceed five years. I know this sounds obvious, but do not have your foreign employee start working before he or she has secured the proper visa. Wait until you have *all* the necessary paperwork in place, not just a signed employment contract. Moving too quickly can cause your employee to be fined, lose his or her job, or even to be deported. The employer can be hit with a much larger fine and be ordered to bear all costs in connection with removing the illegal worker. Serial violators can even lose their ability to hire foreigners under any circumstance.

In 2014, China started drafting a regulation called the Provisions on the Administration of Foreigners Working in China. This regulation is intended to focus on attracting more foreign talent to China. The goal is to replace the current Provisions on the Employment of Foreigners in China, which was promulgated by the Ministry of Human Resources and Social Security in 1995 and recently amended in 2011. Note the interesting change of words from "employment" to "working." This is intentional and was done to deal with how foreign self-employed individuals can legally work in China, not just be employed. The rule is not universal in China on this issue. There is nothing in Chinese law *specifically* prohibiting a foreigner from conducting business as a self-employed individual (except for residents from Hong Kong, Taiwan, and Macau, who are explicitly permitted to do so). However, some places, such as Beijing, explicitly prohibit a foreigner from doing so. Registering such a business in those places is impossible.

CHINA PART-TIME EMPLOYEES: THE 101

As a China employer, you should have a written employment contract with your part-time employees,[30] even though Chinese labor laws do not require it, for the reasons set forth below.

First, the rules in your locale (e.g., Shanghai) may **require** you to have a written contract if your part-time employee requests one, so you may as well be prepared. Being able to present a contract to your potential hire shows you are prepared and know how things work in China. If your employee becomes convinced that you (a foreign employer) don't know how Chinese employment laws work, you could be setting yourself up for future problems. Chinese employees file more grievances against foreign employers than against Chinese employers, especially those that they perceive as not understanding China.

Second, a written contract can be used to make your part-time employee's work responsibilities and obligations clear. Performance issues are more likely to arise when your employee is unclear about what he or she has been hired to do.

Third, written contracts are the best way for you to protect your confidential information, trade secrets, and intellectual property from

---

[30] http://www.chinalawblog.com/2014/08/china-part-time-employee-rules.html

exposure by your employee, part-time or otherwise. A written contract **and** an enforceable damages clause[31] written to deter your part-time employee from stealing your IP, trade secrets, or confidential information can go a long way toward preventing your employee from taking these things to his or her next employer.

If it's not done correctly, however, a written employment contract can backfire. For example, under China's Labor Contract Law, a part-time employee can work no more than four hours a day and no more than 24 hours in a week. Most municipalities enforce this. So if your contract with one of your part-time employees provides that he or she must work 35 hours a week, you are at risk of converting that employee to a full-time employee. And that (now) full-time employee could sue you for all the unpaid social insurance benefits you were supposed to pay but never did, and the labor bureau almost certainly will also fine you for having failed to make mandatory social insurance contributions. Even worse, it can suddenly become incredibly difficult or even impossible for you to terminate your employee because not only did your bad contract convert your employee to a full-time worker, but it also was an open-term contract.

If you have any part-time employees or if you plan to hire any part-time employees, you should probably also add a section to your rules and regulations[32] regarding such employees. The reason for this is simple: a China-based employer must provide all of its employees with a copy of the employer rules and regulations, and all of its employees will be subject to these rules and regulations. If you don't make clear that certain company benefits are **not** available to your part-time employees, you are setting up your part-time employees to believe, and then to argue, that they are entitled to those benefits because your rules and regulations essentially say they are. You should also make sure your rules and regulations do not opt your part-time employees out of any mandatory benefits to which they are entitled, such as work-related injury insurance. Be sure to follow each of the formalities and make all the filings required by your local labor

---

[31] http://www.chinalawblog.com/2015/10/the-effective-china-contract-liquidated-damages.html

[32] http://www.chinalawblog.com/2016/04/china-employer-rules-and-regulations-and-why-you-must-have-one.html

authorities. Do not forget: many China labor laws are local,[33] and the laws on part-time employees are certainly no different.

BOTTOM LINE: Part-time employees have their own special issues in China and you ignore them at your peril.

---

[33] http://www.chinalawblog.com/2015/12/china-employment-law-local-and-not-so-simple.html

CHINA EMPLOYEES AND INDEPENDENT CONTRACTORS: THE O2O BUSINESS CARVE-OUT

Despite the many risks, far too many foreign companies engage in pointless gyrations to convince themselves that their relationship with their China "agent" or "independent contractor" or "partner" is anything other than an employer-employee relationship. Yes, the costs of hiring an employee in China are high, but you have to trust us when we say the costs of improperly trying to get around this in China will almost certainly be much higher. For just how bad this can get, I urge you to check out this Forbes Magazine article, China's Tax Authorities Want You.[34]

But now that I have scared you, I should note that China recently opened the door a crack to allow independent contractor[35]-like relationships in the "online to offline" (O2O[36]) world.

In a series of cases concerning ride-hailing service drivers (think Uber, Lyft, or Didi[37]), China's courts held that the drivers were *not*

---

[34] http://www.forbes.com/sites/danharris/2015/05/28/chinas-tax-authorities-want-you/#3a417d77f540
[35] https://en.wikipedia.org/wiki/Independent_contractor
[36] http://www.investopedia.com/terms/o/onlinetooffline-commerce.asp

employees. In each case, the driver and the company entered into an e-ride-hailing driver cooperation agreement.

Let's look at one recent case (decided in 2015). The plaintiff, a ride-hailing driver for Beijing Yi Xin Yi Xing Auto Technology Development Service Co., Ltd. claimed he was an employee of Yi Xin and was paid RMB 4000 (about USD 600) per month during the term of his employment. But Yi Xin failed to make social insurance payments, withheld his wages, and terminated his employment without cause. The former driver initiated a labor arbitration claim against Yi Xin, demanding (among other things) double statutory severance pay for illegal termination of an employee relationship. The former driver lost at arbitration and then took his case to court, where he lost again. The former driver then appealed to the intermediate court and lost yet again.

The intermediate court held that the former driver bore the burden to prove[38] he had been in an employment relationship with Yi Xin and he had failed to meet that legal burden. The court's analysis is unsatisfactorily brief. It says that in seeking to determine whether an employment relationship existed between the parties, it will consider the following: (1) whether the employer and the employee qualified as employer and employee for purposes of the Chinese labor and employment laws; (2) whether the employee was subject to the employer's rules and regulations and the labor management of the employer and undertook work arrangements from the employer for remuneration; and (3) whether the employee's services constituted a part of the employer's business. The court's ruling did not discuss (1), but I note it generally means the employer must be a China entity with a business license, and the employee must be at least 18 years old. The court went on to say that the parties signed a cooperation agreement, pursuant to which the former driver provided ride-hailing services to clients and charged fees accordingly. Yi Xin then deducted information service fees from the service fees held by the former driver. The former driver worked flexible hours based on his own desires and Yi Xin did not pay him a fixed monthly wage. Therefore, the characteristics of an employment relationship were lacking and no employment relationship existed between the parties. In reaching its

[37] https://en.wikipedia.org/wiki/Didi_Chuxing
[38] https://en.wikipedia.org/wiki/Legal_burden_of_proof

conclusion, the court focused on the former driver's flexible schedule and how he did not take orders from Yi Xin.

In a case currently pending in Chaoyang District People's Court in Beijing, seven chefs brought a legal action against Lekuai Information Technology Co., LTD for unlawful termination. The main issue in their case is the same as that in Yi Xin's case above: did an employment relationship exist between the parties? Much like the arguments made by Yi Xin, the defendant in this case, Lekuai, claimed that it was in "a cooperation relationship" with these chefs, and not an employment relationship. Lekuai further asserts that the parties had agreed in their written "cooperation agreement" that "there was a business cooperation relationship between the parties" and the chefs would *not* be subject to Lekuai labor management and the chefs themselves would be solely responsible for their work product.

These cases do not abrogate the need for foreign companies doing business in China to treat pretty much every individual that performs services for them as an employee and to pay all the taxes and benefits[39] that go with that. In any employee-like dispute, China will no doubt continue to favor the individual against the company, and this holds double for foreign companies. But in an O2O context, it certainly appears that China is loosening the employer-employee strings and its courts are no longer treating all situations where employee-like individuals have independence and flexibility as do traditional employees. Note that the courts did not use the concept "independent contractor" as we commonly see in the U.S.

This could be huge. No employment relationship means the company is *not* obligated to treat the cooperating party as an employee, thereby saving large amounts on labor costs, such as employer taxes, social insurance, and housing fund payments. Termination will also be considerably easier. But what all this means (if anything at all) for China employers outside of the O2O context remains to be seen.

BOTTOM LINE: if you regulate someone pursuant to your company's rules and regulations, the chances are an employment relationship exists between you and such employee. But if you are an O2O

---

[39] http://www.forbes.com/sites/danharris/2015/05/28/chinas-tax-authorities-want-you/#2a7483847f54

company, and if you have a written contract (in Chinese) that clearly delineates in multiple ways that the role of your cooperating individual is not that of employee, you will have a good basis for claiming that person is not an employee. If you want to be really safe though, you should consider requiring that your cooperating individual form his or her own Chinese domestic company and then have your company contract with that company. The number of Chinese domestic companies being formed is rising rapidly as those formations become considerably easier and cheaper.

But whatever you do, do not confuse the above cases with China's flexible working hours system,[40] nor should you forget that foreigners still need a proper work visa to stay and work in China. Most important, if you are going to try to set up a cooperation relationship to avoid an employer-employee relationship, be sure you are documenting it correctly *and in Chinese.*

---

[40] http://www.chinalawblog.com/2014/08/chinas-forty-hour-work-week-is-mandatory-except-when-its-not-part-iii.html

Hiring Employees from Hong Kong, Macau, and Taiwan

Generally speaking, residents of Hong Kong, Macau, and Taiwan may be employed in China if they satisfy the following conditions:

1. They are between the ages of 18 and 60 (subject to a couple of exceptions noted below).
2. They are in good health.
3. They hold a valid mainland travel permit (issued by the PRC Ministry of Public Security).
4. For certain occupations, they must also possess a qualification certificate in accordance with any applicable rules.

As mentioned above, the age requirement may be relaxed if the individual is an investor who will directly participate in the business operation, or if the candidate is a technical person immediately needed in mainland China.

The employer needs to apply to the local labor bureau for an employment permit, usually by submitting the following documents:

1. A copy of the employer's business license.
2. A health certificate (issued by the port hospital of the relevant entry and exit inspection and quarantine department).
3. A letter of intent or a labor contract with the employee (even though a letter of intent will usually suffice, we recommend

you have a written employee agreement with the employee) or other document that can prove the employment relationship.

4. Any applicable professional qualification certificate.
5. The employee's valid mainland travel permit.

The labor bureau will usually make a determination within 10 working days after receipt of all necessary application materials. Just make sure you do it the right way.

DON'T GET LAZY WITH YOUR CHINA EMPLOYMENT CONTRACTS

China's laws protect China's employees. They really, really do.

China law mandates written employment contracts with **all** (Chinese and expat) full-time employees. Those employment contracts must include the following provisions:

- Basic information about the employer and the employee, including place of work;

- Duration of the contract;

- A description of the work the employee will be performing;

- Working hours and rest and leave time;

- Wages and social insurance;

- Applicable labor protections and labor conditions and protection against occupational hazards;

- "Other matters required by relevant laws and regulations."

If an employer goes more than a month without a valid written employment contract with an employee, the employer will be required to pay that employee *double* the employee's monthly wage. If a second one-month period passes without a valid written employment contract (even if the employee refuses to enter into a written contract), the employer must pay applicable economic compensation upon terminating that employee. In addition to the double wages the employer must pay to its employee, most local authorities also fine the employer (sometimes substantially) for having violated the rules on written contracts.

If an employer goes more than a year without a written employment contract with an employee, the employee lacking the written employment contract will be deemed to have entered into an open-term labor contract with the employer, which essentially means there is no definitive end date to the labor relationship. If this happens, it becomes nearly impossible to terminate the employee without having to pay multiple years of wages.

Note that the above rules on double-wage penalty apply to both Chinese and foreign employees working in China. Also be aware that some Chinese labor arbitration commissions and some Chinese courts do not recognize anything other than Chinese language agreements as valid written employment contracts.

Now consider this common situation about which our China lawyers are often contacted. The employer and an employee execute a fixed-term written employment agreement. After that contract expires, the employer and the employee do not renew the contract, but the employee continues working for the employer. The employer just assumes that its previous written contract is in effect and that it and the employee have orally agreed to continue it. But can the employer be penalized for not having a written labor contract with the employee? None of China's national employment rules provide clear guidance on this issue and so (like so many China employment law issues) the answer depends on the employer's location.

The Beijing Labor Bureau is of the clear opinion that an employee who keeps working after a written contract has expired has no valid written contract. This means that the employer must pay **double** the employee's monthly wage for all work performed after the initial written agreement expired. So if you are employing anyone in Beijing under anything other than a still-valid written employment contract, you can (and almost certainly will) eventually get hit with a double-wage penalty for continuing to employ that person after his or her labor contract has expired. This comes as a most unpleasant shock to those to whom this has happened. Though most cities are less clear than Beijing regarding double wages, our China lawyers are aware of companies outside Beijing that either have paid a double-wage penalty or paid settlements with employees as though the double-wage penalty were a real possibility.

BOTTOM LINE: if you are employing anyone in China without an up-to-date contract written in Chinese, you are at risk for a substantial penalty.

CHINA EMPLOYMENT CONTRACTS: IF YOURS ARE NOT CURRENT, YOU HAVE A PROBLEM. THE SHANGHAI VERSION.

To avoid steep penalties, you need a CURRENT written employment agreement (in Chinese) with your employees.

As discussed in China Employment Contracts: If Yours Are Not Current, You Have A Problem,[41] Beijing employers with employees who continue working after the initial labor contract expires will be severely penalized for not having a written labor contract with the employee. Since Shanghai and Beijing often do not see eye to eye on employment matters (Beijing is generally more pro-employee than Shanghai), I thought it would be interesting to compare the way these two cities treat an employee who continues working after his or her written contract has expired. Not surprisingly, Shanghai's position is not as cut and dried as Beijing's. In Shanghai, the principle of good faith governs, and the labor arbitration commission/court should base its decision on the specific circumstances that led to the lack of a written contract.

---

[41] http://www.chinalawblog.com/2015/05/china-employment-contracts-if-yours-are-not-current-you-have-a-problem.html

Pursuant to the Circular of the Supreme People's Court of Shanghai on the Issuance of Opinions Regarding Several Issues Concerning the Application of the Labor Contract Law, the court will consider whether the employer fulfilled its obligation to consult with the employee in good faith, and whether the employee refused to sign the agreement after the employer provided him/her with such a document. Further, the court will not impose a double-wage penalty on the employer if it determines that the employer acted in good faith and that the absence of a written contract was solely the employee's fault or based on a situation completely out of the employer's control (e.g., force majeure[42]).

Another judicial document, Answers of the Supreme People's Court of Shanghai to Several Questions Regarding Labor Disputes, offers additional guidance. It provides that if there is evidence that the employee acted in bad faith and was the reason no written contract was executed, the employer will not be penalized for the employee's wrongdoing. One example of such wrongdoing is an employee who tricks his or her employer into believing that the employee executed a labor contract when, in fact, the employee had someone else sign the contract, thus causing the employer to "fail" to execute a contract with the employee in question. Moreover, if the employer can prove that the reason it cannot produce signed contracts as evidence is because company managers or human resources managers hid the contracts, the employer can still avoid the double-wage penalty by providing other evidence showing that the parties did in fact execute contracts.

BOTTOM LINE: just as in Beijing, smart employers never ever, ever let an employee stay employed without a signed written contract in Chinese. In Shanghai, however, the employer at least has some small chance of avoiding steep penalties for no written contract if the employer can prove that it acted in good faith.

---

[42] https://en.wikipedia.org/wiki/Force_majeure

CHINA EMPLOYMENT LAW: A MEMO ON THE PRACTICALITIES

While cleaning out my computer recently, I came across this memo from one of our China lawyers (who does a substantial amount of China employment law work) to a client. I gave it a quick read and near as I can tell most of it is current. The only things I would note are that the rules can and do vary from province to province and from city to city, and that in some cities it is relatively easy to secure permission to have your employee work without having to pay overtime.

*****

I am writing in response to your recent email regarding [our company's] China employment matters. The basic response to your questions on PRC employment law are as follows. As you can see, the regulations are quite complex. Please contact me if you would like more detail on these matters, or if you have other related questions.

1. In general terms, Chinese law does not allow for "comp time."
Calculation of work time and payment is regulated under the PRC Labor Law. Article 36 of the Labor Law provides for an 8-hour workday and a 44-hour workweek. Article 44 of the Labor Law provides that any labor performed in excess of the statutory amount must be compensated at 150% of the base salary. If the employee

works on a normal rest day (Saturday afternoon or Sunday), then pay is 200% of base. If the employee works on a national holiday, pay is 300% of base. It is not permitted to make up for excess time worked by providing time off in the following week. The statute is silent about adjusting work hours within the same week and many companies will say that if an employee worked 12 hours on day one, that employee can then work 4 hours on day two. Though this is a somewhat common practice, particularly among Chinese companies, this system violates the rules. Under the strict interpretation of the rules, if an employee works 12 hours, 8 hours is at base pay and 4 hours must be paid as overtime. For these reasons, most WFOEs have a very strict rule limiting overtime work. That is, no employee is permitted to work overtime without specific written permission. "Comp time" systems are generally not used in China by foreign companies because they violate the rules and we do not recommend our clients use such a system.

2. Chinese labor law recognizes that for certain types of employment, a regular, 44-hour workweek, 8-hour day simply is not practical.

For example, employees who work in transportation (on trains for example) and employees who work as travel guides will never work a standard week or day. For such employees, permission can be fairly easily obtained from the local labor bureau to establish a system of flexible work hours and accumulation of hours system. This permission system is regulated by the Labor Bureau Method for Enterprise Application for Non-Specified Work Hours and Gross Accumulation of Hours.

Under this system, a company can work with its employees to design a system where hours are accumulated within a week or month in a flexible way that fits with the actual demands of the job. However, the basic rule of this system is that the final result must be as close as practical to a 44-hour workweek and an 8-hour workday. This system cannot be used to impose a non-hourly work system where the employee is paid a monthly salary and is required to work as many hours as are required to get the job done. That is, this system cannot be used to impose a salaried employee system as an hourly employee system. There is no concept of salaried employee under the Chinese labor law system. There is only the method described here where the hourly system is adjusted in a way to accommodate employees who have irregular work hours as an inherent part of their jobs.

Consider the application of the above to your employees. Many of your sales employees will travel. You have two choices that comply with the law. First, absent special permission, you are required to pay overtime for every hour in excess of 8 hours that the employee works, even in cases where the excess hours are caused by travel that cannot be avoided. Second, if this is an excessive burden, you can request permission from your local labor bureau to implement a flexible system to allow for excess time on certain days to be made up as soon as possible by time off on other days, provided that the result is as close to an 8 hour day, 44 hour work week as possible. In general, the employees must agree to this system: it cannot simply be imposed by the employer.

3. You have asked about the system for paying your general manager.

This question applies to management employees in general. What you are really asking is whether or not you can pay your management people using the standard U.S. salaried employee approach. As noted above, the legal regime in China does not recognize the salaried employee concept. This means that for you to avoid paying overtime to your management personnel, you will need to obtain approval from the local labor bureau for an alternative payment system for these employees. However, as I have stated, the rules do not allow for an open-ended, salaried employee approach. Rather, the rules are designed to deal with workers whose jobs require an irregular hourly pattern of work. The rules quite specifically exclude the concept of open-ended work as long as it takes to get the job done systems of compensation. For this reason, applications to impose this kind of salaried employee system are generally not granted by the local labor bureaus, but this does very much depend on the specific local labor bureau.

This whole approach is, of course, not consistent with the way modern companies are managed. The Chinese labor law system does not make any distinction between the factory line worker and the president of the company that owns the factory. By law, and absent approval, both the line worker and the president must be paid using the same rigid hourly wage system. The fact that this is entirely unrealistic means that most companies in China simply ignore the rule for management employees and for sales and other employees who inherently work irregular hours.

However, simply ignoring the law is not a sound strategy for foreign owned companies. When the law is ignored, the result is that the company is subject to large overtime claims from disaffected management and sales employees, and we see this happen all the time after an employee has left the company or is terminated. This issue arises quite consistently when foreign companies terminate a management-level employee. It is an unpleasant shock when the company learns that the manager it just terminated has been carefully accounting for unpaid overtime all along and insists on getting paid all back overtime wages, plus interest on those wages, plus penalties, all in addition to a claim for an already large settlement payment.

4. The Chinese labor law system for vacation time is regulated by the Regulations for Employee Vacation with Pay. Article 3 of these rules provides that vacation with pay is mandatory, in accord with the number of years of employment, according to the following schedule:

— 1 year to 10 years employment: 5 days' vacation.
— 10 years to 20 years employment: 10 days' vacation.
— Over 20 years employment: 15 days' vacation.

Article 5 provides that vacation must be taken in the year accrued. That is, vacation cannot be accumulated and rolled into subsequent years. If the company cannot provide vacation due to the needs of the company, then the company must pay 300% of base salary for every vacation day denied.

Most foreign owned companies have a vacation policy more generous than required by Chinese statute. It is permissible to impose any vacation policy more generous than the Chinese required system, but not one that is less generous. The most contentious area is accrual of vacation. In general, it is considered permissible to allow for accrual and rollover of vacation time if this is the specific desire of the employee. You should note, however, that the regulation is silent on this issue. The Chinese government is concerned that employers will pressure their employees not to take vacation and to accrue the time when this is not really the intent of the employee. Therefore, the regulation favors payment of the 300% of salary as a way to control the actions of the employer.

Most employers simply use whatever U.S. vacation policy they have in place as their policy for China, though this is not always the best plan. It is better to adopt a vacation policy that complies with the Chinese system, with additional benefits on top of the Chinese system if that is considered desirable. Note also that the vacation policy should apply to *all* employees. Some companies will apply the policy only to management personnel. This is not acceptable under Chinese law.

5. Many Chinese-owned companies ignore the requirements of the Employment Law and the associated regulations.

It is therefore common for Chinese staff of foreign owned companies to recommend that you too ignore the rules. However, this is not a good strategy for foreign companies. When a complaint is raised, the local labor bureaus are quite aggressive in enforcing the strict requirements of the labor system against foreign owned companies and this type of enforcement is becoming *more* common, not less. Accordingly, even when the rules are difficult to deal with, you must be sure to follow them as closely as possible. Also, the employee who told you not to follow the rules will not hesitate to sue you for not following the rules, when doing so suits his or her purpose later down the road.

CHINA EMPLOYMENT CONTRACTS: WHY OURS ARE IN CHINESE

Our China lawyers sometimes get "simple" questions from our WFOE clients regarding China's labor law. One such question is whether they must use Chinese as the prevailing language for their labor contracts with their employees, especially with their expat employees. This question is not as simple as it may first appear.

First off, there is little national guidance on this other than an "ancient" 1995 document with the long title of Letter of the General Office of the Ministry of Labor on Implementation of the Regulation on the Labor Administration of Enterprises with Foreign Investment (the "Letter"). The Letter explicitly requires that the language of a China labor contract be in Chinese. However, the authority of this document is questionable because its underlying regulation is no longer in effect, having been replaced in 2007 by the PRC Labor Law and other relevant laws and regulations. So just as is the case with so much of employment law in China, it is important to look into how each locale deals with this issue.

In Shanghai, you must have a Chinese version for your labor contract. Though you **may** have an English language translation of your contract, Chinese **must** be the controlling language. Shanghai (more so than many other Chinese cities) generally takes a liberal view on freedom of contract and when it comes to labor contracts between

Shanghai employers and their expat employees, Shanghai generally will respect the parties' own arrangement so long as those terms do not contradict matters covered in the relevant laws. Notwithstanding Shanghai's general approach, if there is a conflict between a Chinese language employment contract and an English language version, the Chinese version will control.

Similarly, Jiangsu Province explicitly states in its provincial Labor Contract Regulations that in the event of a dispute involving an employment contract written in a foreign language and in Chinese, the Chinese language will prevail.

What happens in legal disputes where the employment contract is only in English? The courts will sometimes have the contract translated, but other times they will simply rule that there is no valid employment contract and penalize the employer accordingly.

BOTTOM LINE: We recommend inserting a provision into your labor contract making it clear that the Chinese language will control. We make this recommendation because the Chinese language version almost certainly will be the one that applies anyway, but also because this lets everyone know exactly what will happen if there is any dispute regarding the applicable language — and disputes happen more often than you would think.

For our clients, we virtually always write their employment contracts in both English and Chinese, even though the Chinese will control. We do this because it is critical that our clients fully understand their employment contracts (and with that, the company rules and regulations relating to their employees) so they can be sure to abide by them. Employer-employee disputes are incredibly common in China, particularly for foreign companies doing business in China. Having clearly written employment contracts in both Chinese and in English can go a long way toward reducing those disputes.

You might also want to check out this post (from way back in 2009), China OEM Agreements. Why Ours Are In Chinese.[43] Flat Out. It discusses why — for similar reasons — we typically write our OEM manufacturing agreements in Chinese as well.

---

[43] http://www.chinalawblog.com/2009/07/china_oem_agreements_we_like_o.html

DO NOT TRY THIS AT HOME

I had a conversation recently with the in-house counsel for a relatively small American company who took crazy risks by writing his company's own China employment contracts, even though he clearly is not himself a China lawyer, nor does he have any real experience with China law. I had the following issues with what he had done:

1. He speaks no Chinese, so whatever he wrote would need to be translated into Chinese (I am going to assume that he at least did this). Unless he hired an experienced Chinese employment lawyer to do the translation, the odds that the translation will actually work are about 10,000 to 1.

2. I wish I had asked him whether he also drafted the Rules and Regulations for his company's China employees. A China employment contract without Rules and Regulations is of virtually no value for a company. I'm betting that he did not.

3. Did his employment contract and Rules and Regulations include provisions regarding the FCPA, China anti-corruption laws, expense reimbursements, education reimbursements, housing reimbursements, overtime, vacations, bonuses, trade secrets, non-competes, etc.? If they did, what in the world made this lawyer think he knew how any of these are supposed to work in China?

4. Did he check with the local labor bureau to determine its position on various employment law matters? These labor bureaus are all over the

map on countless employment issues, and the positions of these labor bureaus truly matter. I am virtually certain he did not.

As our lead China employment lawyer, Grace spends several hours each week keeping up to date with China's employment laws and regulations and maintaining strong contacts with local labor bureaus throughout China. She has conveyed a small portion of that knowledge via the following China employment law posts:

- Paying Your Non-Chinese Employees In Your China WFOE: Splitting The Salary, Part 1[44]
- Paying Your Non-Chinese Employees In Your China WFOE: Splitting The Salary Part 2[45]
- China's Forty Hour Work Week Is Mandatory. Except When It's Not.[46]
- China's Forty Hour Work Week Is Mandatory. Except When It's Not. Part II[47]
- China's Forty Hour Work Week Is Mandatory. Except When It's Not. Part III[48]
- China Part-Time Employee Rules[49]
- China Employment Offer Letters: Be Careful[50]
- China Employee Probation: Don't Let It Slip Away[51]
- China Non-Competes. Oh, Oh, The Price You'll Pay[52]

---

[44] http://www.chinalawblog.com/2014/02/paying-your-non-chinese-employees-in-your-china-wfoe-splitting-the-salary-part-1.html

[45] http://www.chinalawblog.com/2014/02/paying-your-non-chinese-employees-in-your-china-wfoe-splitting-the-salary-part-2.html

[46] http://www.chinalawblog.com/2014/06/chinas-forty-hour-work-week-is-mandatory-except-when-its-not.html

[47] http://www.chinalawblog.com/2014/06/chinas-forty-hour-work-week-is-mandatory-except-when-its-not-part-ii.html

[48] http://www.chinalawblog.com/2014/08/chinas-forty-hour-work-week-is-mandatory-except-when-its-not-part-iii.html

[49] http://www.chinalawblog.com/2014/08/china-part-time-employee-rules.html

[50] http://www.chinalawblog.com/2014/08/china-employment-offer-letters-be-careful.html

[51] http://www.chinalawblog.com/2014/09/china-employee-probation-dont-let-it-slip-away.html

[52] http://www.chinalawblog.com/2014/09/china-non-competes-oh-oh-the-price-youll-pay.html

- China Employee Leaving Employment Early. Forget About Payment In Lieu Of Notice[53]
- Your China Expat Employee Contract. It Depends....[54]
- China Employee Vacations: Don't Stop Them. Just Don't[55]

Please understand that reading each of the above posts will not give you the knowledge you need to draft a China employee contract, just as reading a medical book or two does not qualify you to perform surgery.

So what is "really" involved in drafting China employment contracts?

Below is the email we send to clients that retain us to draft China employment contracts for their China WFOE, setting out the initial information we need to get started on drafting their employee contracts and Rules and Regulations.

I. Basic Information. Please provide the following information:

— **A.** Name and registered address of the WFOE,[56] in English and Chinese.

— **B.** A one paragraph statement of: 1) the number of employees, 2) the duties and title of each employee, 3) the pay scale/rate for each employee, and 4) the nationality of each employee.

— **C.** The hours that you expect each employee to work. Standard working hours in most parts of China[57] follow a 40-hour workweek: 8 hours a day and 5 days a week. If you anticipate any significant exceptions to that, please explain.

---

[53] http://www.chinalawblog.com/2014/09/china-employee-leaving-employment-early-forget-about-payment-in-lieu-of-notice.html

[54] http://www.chinalawblog.com/2014/10/your-china-expat-employee-contract-it-depends.html

[55] http://www.chinalawblog.com/2014/10/china-employee-vacations-dont-stop-them-just-dont.html

[56] http://www.chinalawblog.com/2009/12/how_to_start_a_business_in_chi.html

[57] http://www.chinalawblog.com/2012/02/overtime_pay_in_china_what_ya_gonna_do.html

— **D.** The name and title of the person who will execute the employee agreements on behalf of the WFOE. Usually, the WFOE's general manager will execute all employee agreements except for his or her own, which will be executed by the WFOE's legal representative.

II. Employee-Specific Information

— **A. Required Information**. For each employee, please provide the following information:

a. The employee's name and title, in English and Chinese.

b. The employee's registered permanent address, in English and Chinese.

c. The employee's contact address (if different from the above), in English and Chinese.

d. The employee's phone number and email address.

e. The employee's national ID number. I recommend getting a scan of the national ID card itself.

f. The employee's gender, citizenship, and date of birth.

g. The employee's place of work, if different from the WFOE address, in both English and Chinese.

h. The term of the employment agreement, including the start date.

i. The amount of wages during the standard employment term, converted into a monthly wage.

j. The date that wages will be paid during the standard employment term.

k. Whether the employee will be paid on a 12-month or 13-month schedule (more on this below).

l. The term of the probation period.

m. The wages during the probation period, converted into a monthly wage.

n. Whether you would like to explore the possibility of an alternative working hours system (that is, an alternative to the standard of 5 days/week, 8 hours/day). The availability of this option will depend on the employee's title and job duties.

o. Whether you would like to explore the possibility of a non-compete agreement (more on this below).

p. Whether you would like to have an education reimbursement agreement (more on this below).

q. The employee's relevant bank account information.

— B. Employment Term and Probation Period. The term of the probation period is roughly proportional to the term of the agreement. The maximum probation period is 6 months. To have a maximum-length probation period, an employment agreement must have a term of at least 3 years. Before the end of the probation period, you can terminate the employee without having to pay severance if you can prove the employee has failed to meet your recruitment requirements. At the end of the initial employment term, you can terminate the employee and pay severance or you can sign the employee to another agreement.

We will need to confirm with the labor bureau in your specific city, but in most Chinese cities, once you have engaged the employee for two terms, when the third term starts, you are required to retain the employee up to mandatory retirement age. Termination during that period requires good cause.

The probation period should be treated seriously and no employee should be taken beyond the probation period unless you are certain that he or she will work out under the terms of this employee agreement. For new employees, we generally recommend a term of three years and a probation period of six months. Many of our foreign clients choose to do an initial term of only one year, and most end up regretting that decision.

— C. Monthly Salary. As noted above, you will need to convert each employee's annual salary into a monthly wage. In many parts of China, it is customary to pay the salary on a 13-month basis, with the final month paid just prior to the Chinese New Year. Either approach is acceptable, but it is important to state clearly in the contract what you will be doing. Many employees expect a "New Year's Bonus" and failure to pay it (if expected) can cause problems. This expectation varies by the industry (manufacturing vs. office work), the type of employees (blue collar vs. white collar), and the geographic location (north vs. south). Note that paying on a 13-month basis does not obligate you to pay more in salary; you would just divide the annual salary by 13 instead of 12.

III. Documents To Be Drafted

Our standard employment package includes the following documents:

—A. Universal Documents

a. Labor Contract. The employment agreement to be used with all employees, with different options selected with respect to the employee's working location, the availability of alternative working hours systems, the length of the probation period, and the term of the agreement itself.

Because the employment rules vary from city to city in China, we will work with you and/or your HR department to go over the above issues and determine how to tailor the initial set of agreements.

b. Trade Secrecy and Intellectual Property Protection Agreement. Self-explanatory, but tailored for use in China. We can further customize it if you have specific confidentiality policies or procedures.

c. Rules and Regulations. This is a long and complex document that is basically a handbook on Chinese labor law. China is not an at-will employment jurisdiction. Employees are employed subject to contract and can be terminated only if they violate that contract. The rules and regulations set out the full set of terms that govern the employment relationship. Most of the content in this document is required by Chinese law and is therefore not optional. We can do some customization of this document, but not much.

d. Confirmation of Receipt. A one-page document stating that the employee has received and understood the contents of the Rules and Regulations.

— B. Optional Documents

a. Non-competition Agreement. Chinese law allows for non-compete agreements,[58] but the terms are restricted as follows:

- As a general rule, only certain staff (senior management, senior technicians, and other personnel who have a confidentiality obligation) may be covered.

- The term is limited to two years.

- Compensation must be paid to the employee during the entire term of restriction. The amount of compensation is not defined by law, but many cities have de facto rules.

Let us know if you are interested in non-competition agreements[59] for any of your employees.

b. Education Reimbursement Agreement. This agreement would be applicable in the following scenario: you pay major expenses for an employee's employment-related education or training, but after the training is complete, the employee quits. In such a situation, you can require that the employee reimburse your company for the education expenses. To do this, however, you must first have in place a written education reimbursement agreement.

Let us know if you are interested in education reimbursement agreements for any of your employees.

Note that though our employment agreements contain basic anti-corruption language, they are *not* a substitute for a full-fledged China compliance program.[60]

---

[58] http://www.chinalawblog.com/2014/09/china-non-competes-oh-oh-the-price-youll-pay.html

[59] http://www.chinalawblog.com/2014/09/how-to-terminate-a-china-employee-non-compete-agreement-very-carefully.html

[60] http://www.chinalawblog.com/2014/08/china-compliance-dont-rely-on-your-china-staff-part-iv.html

CHINA EMPLOYEE LEAVING EMPLOYMENT EARLY: FORGET ABOUT PAYMENT IN LIEU OF NOTICE

China allows employees to terminate labor contracts by giving 30 days' written notice to the employer during the standard employment term or three days' written notice during the probation period.

Our clients occasionally ask us whether it is permissible under Chinese law to require an employee to pay a certain amount of money (代通知金 or 代替通知金) to an employer, when the employee tries to terminate the labor contract without prior written notice. We have received inconsistent responses from a few cities' labor bureaus, but it seems the majority think that would be illegal, and putting such a provision into an employment contract would be illegal as well.

To be clear, the phrase "代通知金" is nowhere to be found in China's Labor Contract Law. The concept does exist in the Law though: for example, Article 40 provides a list of circumstances under which an employer may terminate an employee without cause but must either give a 30 days' written notice or payment of an additional month's salary to the terminated employee.

As mentioned above, it seems that payment in lieu of notice may only be applied to an employer, and that requiring an employee to pay in lieu of notice is not in line with PRC labor laws. One major reason is that China's Labor Contract Law was intended to make it relatively easy for employees to terminate labor contracts. Employees should be able to get out of an employment relationship simply by giving prior written notice and, perhaps more important, they should be able to do so without a penalty. Therefore, any additional obligation on the part of the employee would violate the spirit of the law, even if the employee has some choice in the matter.

Some practitioners also believe that an employee "payment in lieu of notice" constitutes a penalty under Chinese laws, which are fairly strict about when an employer can impose a penalty on an employee. Specifically, China's Labor Contract Law allows only the following two circumstances when an employer and an employee can agree on a penalty provision payable by the employee.

- Pursuant to an education reimbursement agreement, an employer can require that the employee reimburse the company for the education expenses if the company pays major expenses for an employee's employment-related education or training, but after the training is complete, the employee quits.
- Pursuant to a non-compete provision or agreement, an employer can require that an employee pay a penalty to the company if the employee violates any non-compete terms by, for example, joining a competitor after leaving employment.

China's Labor Contract Law makes clear that except for the two circumstances above, an employer and an employee may not agree on any provision that requires the employee to pay a penalty to the employer.

BOTTOM LINE: the safest thing for you to do as an employer is to require that your employees give 30 days' prior written notice during the standard employment term, and three days' written notice during the probation period for early termination of a labor contract, and not to provide or take money in lieu of that.

HIRING A CHINA EMPLOYEE THROUGH A DISPATCH COMPANY: DON'T FORGET ABOUT YOUR IP

Despite the increasing restrictions on using employee dispatch companies for hiring of "your" China employees, our China lawyers have seen very little in the way of a slowdown in smaller companies choosing to go that route, especially if doing so will allow them to delay for that much longer having to form a China WFOE.

The legal issues for foreign companies that use employee dispatch companies are not terribly complicated, with one exception.

The way the whole system works is that you, as the foreign company, sign a contract with the employee dispatch company for it to hire, as its own employee, an individual or individuals you would like to work for your company. The better dispatch companies generally have pretty good contracts for this and so our role as attorneys for our foreign clients is mostly to point out the provisions over which our clients have some negotiating power.

The complication arises in the contract between the employee dispatch company and its/your employee, and it is here where we see the most mistakes made. The employee dispatch company drafts its employment contract with its/your employee to protect and benefit itself, without any real regard for you. In most respects, your interests are fairly well lined up with the employee dispatch company, and so for the most part it is a good thing that most of these companies draft good China employee contracts.

But when it comes to your intellectual property, you need to account for the fact that your employee dispatch company does not care at all. And when I say "at all," I mean *at all*. Your employee dispatch company does not care if its contract with its/your employee protects your IP, and your employee dispatch company does not care if its contract fails to protect your IP.

For this reason, you have to care and you have to be the one to make sure that the employee contract reflects this. If you want to be sure that the employee does not end up owning your intellectual property, you need to make sure that the employee contract is clear on this. If you want to be sure that your employee signs a contract that reduces the likelihood that he or she will run off with your trade secrets, you need to make sure that the employee contract has provisions for that.

Because if you do not make sure that your China attorneys do this, nobody else will.

The Basics on Probation

There is some truth to an old expression about China employees, "Once hired, never fired." Terminating a Chinese employee is rarely going to be easy, but if that employee is on probation, you at least have a better chance of not getting sued for doing so.

China allows probationary periods for Chinese employees, but only if done right. The maximum term of the probationary period depends on the term of the employment contract. If the employment contract is for between three months and one year, the probationary period can be for up to one month. If the employment contract is for between one year and three years, the probationary period can be for up to two months. For fixed-term employment contracts of three years or more, and for employment contracts with no fixed term, the probationary period can be for up to six months.

If the employment contract terminates upon completion of an agreed assignment, or if the employment contract is for less than three months, there can be no probationary period.

An employee may be subject to only one probationary period with the same employer – and this holds true even if the employee leaves that employer and then rejoins it.

Any probationary period **must** be set forth in the employment contract. If an employer enters into a separate agreement with its employee for a probationary period, the probationary agreement will be void and there will be no probationary period. The employer will be deemed to have entered into a fixed-term contract with the employee. This is done to prevent an employer who becomes unhappy with its employee from putting that employee on probation after the hiring.

CHINA LAW ON TERM EMPLOYMENT CONTRACTS

One of our clients recently came to the end of its contract term with the bulk of its China employees. The client wrote asking questions regarding fixed-term employment contracts under Chinese law. Here's the full reply, which you might find edifying:

Pursuant to Chinese law, you are permitted to enter into two fixed-term contracts with an employee. The term of these contracts can be any fixed-term that is agreed to between the parties. Typically in China the term ranges from one to five years. At the end of the second fixed-term contract, you have two choices. You can choose not to continue the employment relationship or you can choose to continue the employment relationship under an open-term relationship.

An open-term relationship requires a written contract. This contract has no term. It terminates only under the following circumstances: 1) the employee voluntarily resigns; 2) the employee reaches retirement age; or 3) the employee is terminated for "cause." Termination for cause is complex and difficult in China. There are two basic areas for cause. In the first, the employee has committed a crime like theft or a gross breach of conduct rules, such as arriving to work drunk. In this case, termination is straightforward. In the second, the employee shows up to work on time and follows all the rules, but is simply incompetent. At present, it is virtually impossible to terminate an employee who falls into this second category. Accordingly, you should never enter into an open-ended employment relationship with an employee you suspect will fall into this second category. But that is often hard to predict. In actual practice, there are various ways companies deal with such employees. The reality is that an employee with a "thick face" who is willing to earn minimum wage and engage in dead-end tasks is very difficult to terminate under the current Chinese system.

China's labor laws are new, so many of the issues have not yet been fully worked out. However, the trend is toward increased employee protection and not toward more employer freedom. The trend is the same in Europe, so there is nothing unique about the Chinese approach. China follows a European approach, and that is the place to look for guidance by analogy. The U.S. is NOT the place to look to for guidance; the Chinese system is as different from the U.S. as any system could be.

CHINA EMPLOYEE NON-COMPETES — THE WHO, WHAT, WHEN, WHERE, AND HOW MUCH?

U nder China's labor laws, an employer and an employee may enter into a non-compete agreement or agree on a set of non-compete provisions (usually in the employment agreement or in a confidentiality agreement) that prohibits the employee from competing with the employer for up to two years after the employment term.

WHO CAN BE SUBJECT TO A NON-COMPETE?

China employee non-compete agreements are generally limited to senior management, senior technicians, and other personnel who have a confidentiality obligation. "Senior management" usually means a person in a senior management position with access to the company's confidential information. A "senior technician" usually means someone engaged in technology research and development, and who has fairly comprehensive access to the company's technological information.

Whether an employee falls under the category of "other personnel who have a confidentiality obligation" is determined on a case-by-case basis by considering all relevant facts, including the following:

- The employee's compensation;
- The employee's job title;
- The employee's responsibilities;
- The likelihood of the employee's gaining access to and making use of the confidential information;
- Whether the employee also signed a confidentiality agreement with the employer;
- Whether the employee is suffering a financial hardship in his or her post-employment period and the extent of that hardship.

NON-COMPETE PERIOD

The PRC Labor Contract Law limits the non-compete period to no more than two years. The two-year period starts to run from the time the employment contract ends or is terminated. Some local rules set forth a permissible period longer than this two-year statutory maximum, but the Labor Contract Law must be followed. As our regular readers know, we are always stressing the need to comply with the national, the provincial, and the local laws, and this is especially true with labor laws. See China Employment Law: Local and Not So Simple.[61] It is important, however, to distinguish between a situation where there is no national guidance or the national law is ambiguous or not detailed, and a situation where there is a clear national law and the local rules clearly conflict with the applicable national law. In the latter case, the national law typically prevails. We virtually never say this, but it is almost always best to leave the task of figuring out how to harmonize two or more laws to your China lawyer.

NON-COMPETE COMPENSATION

---

[61] http://www.chinalawblog.com/2015/12/china-employment-law-local-and-not-so-simple.html

In exchange for an employee's promise to uphold a non-compete requirement, the employer is required to pay economic compensation to the employee. An employer's failure to pay the non-compete compensation means the employee can stop abiding by the non-compete provisions.

Under the *Judicial Interpretation IV of the Supreme People's Court on Several Issues Concerning the Application of Law in Hearing Labor Dispute Cases* ("Judicial Interpretation IV"), the amount set forth in an agreement between an employer and an employee regarding post-employment compensation for a non-compete provision will prevail. If the agreement is silent on the amount of post-employment compensation for the non-compete provision, the employer must pay the employee 30% of the employee's average monthly salary in the twelve months before termination, or the local minimum wage, whichever is higher.

Notwithstanding the issuance of *Judicial Interpretation IV*, we are still finding local differences regarding the required amount for non-compete compensation.

One question is whether a non-compete compensation provision will be upheld if the agreed-upon amount is less than the local minimum wage. We have seen a trend among Chinese courts in major cities to strictly enforce contractual non-competes, even when the agreed-upon non-compete compensation is extremely low. However, to avoid doubt and to avoid triggering the default rule, we advise our clients to specify non-compete compensation greater than the local minimum wage.

CONTRACT DAMAGES PROVISION

An employee non-compete agreement is one of the few instances where a China employer is legally allowed to impose a penalty on an employee. This is done via a specific contract damages provision. By agreeing to such a provision, an employee agrees to pay a specific damage amount if he or she fails to comply with the non-compete provision.

The standard is simple: the contract damages must be a good-faith estimate of the employer's damages in advance. If a PRC court or other arbitral body considers your contract damages amount too high, and thus too harsh on your employee (an argument virtually every employee will make), it will reduce this amount or perhaps even eliminate it entirely. For a discussion of the difficulties inherent in coming up with an appropriate contract damages amount, check out China Contract Damages: More Art Than Science.[62]

An employee cannot simply pay contract damages to get out of his or her non-compete obligations. The employer may demand that its employee continue to perform his or her non-compete obligations (provided it is still within the non-compete period) even if the employee has paid contract damages for violating the non-compete agreement.

GEOGRAPHIC SCOPE

The standard here is quite simple: the geographic scope must be "reasonable." In determining what constitutes a reasonable geographic scope for a non-compete, the Chinese courts will consider all facts, including the employer's business scope, the employer's size, the employer's industry, and the employee's position.

It usually makes sense to make your geographic scope as expansive as you deem appropriate because Chinese courts do not usually strike down a non-compete provision simply because its geographic scope is too broad. Instead, they will usually employ what is sometimes called the "blue-pencil doctrine"[63] to reduce the geographic scope of the agreement, but leave it intact. On the flip side, it is nearly impossible to expand the scope of a non-compete in court. This means that you want your non-compete agreement to tilt toward the broad side, but not be so broad that a court throws up its hands and strikes the whole thing.

EARLY TERMINATION

Once the non-compete period has begun, employers cannot terminate a non-compete agreement without being subjected to a penalty.

---

[62] http://www.chinalawblog.com/2015/01/liquidated-damages-in-your-china-contract.html

[63] https://en.wikipedia.org/wiki/Blue_pencil_doctrine

Pursuant to *Judicial Interpretation IV*, employers that unilaterally terminate a non-compete agreement during the non-compete period must pay the employee three additional months of non-compete compensation for the early termination.

Also keep in mind that if you fail to make compensation payments for three months or longer, the employee has the right to unilaterally terminate the non-compete, provided the employee has performed his or her non-compete obligation and is not the cause for the employer's failure to make payments. So if you want your non-compete agreement to remain in force, be sure to pay on it.

CHINA EMPLOYEE NON-COMPETES: DOES YOURS HAVE REAL TEETH?

China employee non-compete[64] agreements and provisions are often litigated. Many employers (wrongly) assume they cannot prevail in these disputes because employees usually win. This belief is not only wrong, but risky. It is wrong because Chinese courts do not automatically side with the employee; rather, those rare employers that have done things the right way usually win. It is also risky because employers with this attitude and approach tend to do an even poorer job of making sure they have a well-crafted contract, are complying with the law, and are preserving good evidence, which are keys to employer success in any employee dispute.

Let's look at a fairly recent case in Guangdong. The employee was hired as a Brand Promotion Manager and was then promoted to project manager. The employee's monthly base salary was low: he started at RMB 3000 per month and it was then raised to RMB 4000 per month, plus commission. The employee signed a three-year employment contract and also executed a confidentiality agreement stating that if he violated any term of the agreement, such as competing with his employer in any way, he would be liable for contract damages of twice his total income during the 12 months

---

[64] http://www.chinalawblog.com/2016/10/china-employee-non-competes-the-who-what-when-where-and-how-much.html

before his termination. There was no agreement on any non-compete compensation. A few months before the employee left his employment, he formed his own company with essentially the same business scope as his employer, and in the same city. The employee was the legal representative of that new company. A few months later, the employer eventually fired the employee and the employee then sued his former employer, demanding unpaid salary and commissions and double severance for wrongful termination.

The procedural history is somewhat messy (with multiple labor arbitrations and lawsuits), but essentially the employee lost in the lower court and then appealed and lost again. The employee then petitioned to the Guangdong Province High People's Court for retrial and lost again.

The primary arguments set forth by the employee were as follows: (1) he was not paid any compensation for not competing, so the non-compete should not be upheld; (2) he was a low-paid ordinary employee with no access to confidential information so the non-compete was never valid in the first place; and (3) the contract damages in the confidentiality agreement were grossly disproportionate to his salary, so requiring him to pay such a large amount would be greatly unfair.

The court decided against the employee on all counts, finding that: (1) the employee had a duty not to compete with his employer during his term of employment, and the employer was not required to pay the employee any compensation for performing the non-compete obligations during such period; (2) the employee signed a confidentiality agreement binding him not to disclose his employer's confidential information and not to compete with his employer; and (3) the employee failed to present any evidence proving the contract damages were so high as to be unfair.

The employee was ordered to pay around 130,000 RMB to his previous employer per the agreed contract damages provision, an amount nearly 33 times his monthly base salary.

There is much to be learned from this case about China employee non-competes, including the following:

1. A non-compete with a fairly low paid employee can be enforceable. The key is more about the position than the pay.

2. Generally speaking, an employer is not required to pay non-compete compensation *during the term of employment.*

3. It is possible to enforce a contract damages provision in an employee non-compete. If you want your non-compete provisions to have real teeth, consider adding an appropriately crafted contract damages provision to your employment contracts that contains a non-compete provision, or to your non-compete agreements.

4. Proving actual damages in a non-compete dispute is usually difficult and this is all the more reason why you should have a contract damages clause in your employment contracts with non-compete provisions, or in your non-compete agreements. See China Contract Damages: More Art than Science,[65] for why contract damages are critical to most China contracts, and for how to determine the proper amount of damages to put into your contract.

5. Before you hire any new employee make sure your potential candidate is not violating a non-compete agreement with his or her previous employer because the last thing you want is for your company to be sued by that previous employer. These sorts of lawsuits are becoming increasingly common in China and the courts are often quick to favor them.

---

[65] http://www.chinalawblog.com/2015/01/liquidated-damages-in-your-china-contract.html

CHINA EMPLOYMENT LAWS: WHAT TO DO WHEN THE EMPLOYMENT RELATIONSHIP ENDS

When the employment relationship ends between a China employer and employee, there are always a few things the China employer should do. One of the most important things you as an employer must do is provide your soon to be ex-employee with a Proof of Termination of Employment Relationship document, transferring the employee's files and social insurance, and completing any other relevant procedures required under the law. Failing to provide such a document gives your ex-employee a near-perfect basis for suing you.

What does this document do? It evidences the termination of your employment relationship. Why do you have to provide this document? Because your employee probably needs it to prove his or her employability. On the flip side, you should require all your new employees to provide you with such a document before you hire them. China employees also need this document to claim unemployment benefits, and if your delay in getting them this document causes them a delay in collecting their unemployment benefits, you are legally responsible for those damages.

Regardless of why the employment relationship has ended, you must perform your legal obligations by providing your former employee with a proof of termination document. It is not relevant that the termination was amicable. Under China's Labor Contract Law, failing to provide this document subjects the employer to both administrative corrective orders and to having to pay the ex-employee any damages suffered because of your failure to follow the law. If you don't want an employee to sue you for his or her inability to get a new job, you should provide this document to all your ex-employees as soon as you possibly can.

This document typically must specify the term of the employment contract, the date when the employment contract was terminated or ended, the position the employee held, and the number of years of the employee was employed. It is important to be careful not to go much beyond this because the more you put in, the more likely it is that what you wrote could backfire on you. Here is just one example: your ex-employee, who is leaving voluntarily, asks you to do them a "favor" by stating in that document that you unilaterally terminated the employment contract, with the excuse being that they do not want to look like a job-hopper. You go along with this and then he or she flips around and sues you for unlawful termination.

Because a well-crafted Proof of Termination of Employment Document is and should be brief, it will not include enough to protect you as the employer. It does not address why the employee left employment. It does not address any statutory severance the employer may owe. Finally, it does not address any future claim the employee might bring. Claims by ex-employees are being brought more and more often, particularly against foreign employers. See China Employment Arbitration: Good Luck with That Battle.[66]

A proof of termination document is primarily done for the benefit of the ex-employee and the next employer, **not for the employer.** For this reason, it usually makes sense for you as the employer to get your departing employees to sign a settlement/severance agreement. Although this agreement can also serve as proof of termination of an employment relationship, it goes beyond that. It should ensure that you will not get sued by your ex-employee one week, one month, or

---

[66] http://www.chinalawblog.com/2016/06/china-employment-arbitration-good-luck-with-that-battle.html

one year down the road. Such an agreement should be explicitly clear that the employee is releasing the employer and any of its affiliates from any future claims that could be brought by the employee. This agreement should be in Chinese (the official language) as well as in English (for your reference). You should not submit this agreement to China's labor authorities. In fact, we usually recommend that it contain hard-hitting confidentiality provisions. You must follow all your internal procedures in having this severance document executed by both parties, and it should also comply with and work under China's employment and contract laws.

BOTTOM LINE: when your China employee walks out your door for the last time – no matter what the circumstances – you as the employer need to do a whole host of things to make sure that you do not see that same employee walking through a court door a few months later.

SECTION TWO

BUMPS IN THE ROAD

A bad thing may become a good thing under certain conditions (塞翁失马, 焉知非福).

~ Huainanzi

CHINA EMPLOYEE MASS LAYOFF LAWS

China's rules on mass layoffs are complicated, localized, and unclear.

It is not news that China's economic growth has been slow. In recent times, we have seen employee layoffs in China by such well-known companies as Lenovo, Samsung, HTC, Yahoo, and Zynga China. This mass layoff trend will no doubt continue even if China manages to quickly shore up its economy, especially in industries such as clothing, electronics, machinery, and furniture. Here are a few of China's basic rules regarding "mass layoffs."

Under China's labor laws, a "mass layoff" is defined as one of the following:

1. An employer reduces its workforce by *twenty* or more employees, **or**
2. An employer reduces its workforce by more than 10% of its entire workforce.

A mass layoff is treated as a unilateral termination by the employer for purposes of Chinese labor law. This means that the employer is usually required to provide severance pay to the employees it terminates. Companies that engage in mass layoffs usually use a "N+1" formula, essentially giving each employee one month's salary for every year he or she worked for the company, plus an additional one month's salary.

Some big companies offer more generous severance pay, sometimes going up to N+6.

Under China's Labor Contract Law, an employer may initiate mass layoffs only under one of the following four circumstances:

1. The employer undergoes a reorganization in accordance with the PRC Enterprise Bankruptcy Law.
2. The employer experiences significant difficulties in its business operation.
3. The employer switches production, makes major technological innovation, adjusts its business model – *and after modifying its labor contracts* – still needs to lay off employees.
4. The employer has experienced other significant changes that modified the economic circumstances that formed the basis for its having signed the labor contracts, and it is unable to perform under the contracts.

A number of the key terms referenced above have been left undefined. For example, the law is silent on what constitutes "significant difficulties in the business operation" and there is no national standard on this. Rather, China arbitration centers and courts generally use local standards in defining "significant difficulties." For example, in Beijing, an employer is deemed to be experiencing "significant difficulties in its business operation" if the following are true:

1. It is "in deficit" for three continuous years.
2. The deficit has increased every year.
3. It is insolvent.
4. 80% of its workforce has stopped working.
5. It cannot pay its employees' living allowances for six continuous months.

It is also unclear what is meant by "other significant changes that modified the economic circumstances." In practice, this usually refers to a situation where the employer switches or stops production, but again (and as is the case with pretty much every aspect of China employment law[67]), the rules on this vary by locale.

At least thirty days before initiating a mass layoff, the employer is required to present a plan to the labor union or to all of its employees (if there is no labor union representing its employees) for reducing its staff. The employer must then consider any comments it might receive from its union or its employees, revise and improve its layoff plan accordingly, and then file a report with the relevant authorities. Even though the law does not specifically say the employer needs to wait until its report has been approved by the labor bureau before it can initiate the layoff process, some places (such as Shanghai) treat the filing requirement as requiring prior government approval. So again, *it is important that you comply with local laws.*

China's Ministry of Human Resources and Social Security recently issued Draft Regulations on Corporate Mass Layoffs. These new rules have never been implemented and so they have not really helped to clarify the process. As things now stand, we generally advise that you follow each of the rules on mass layoffs, and if possible, get each of your terminated employees to sign a China-appropriate settlement and a release agreement as well.

---

[67] http://abovethelaw.com/2015/01/china-employment-law-its-complicated-and-its-localized/

HOW TO AVOID LIFETIME EMPLOYEES

In China, an open-term labor contract is a contract where the employer and its employee agree that there is no definitive ending date for the labor relationship. Such a contract generally means the employer must retain the employee until his or her retirement age, though the employee can terminate at any time, with no restriction or penalty.

The PRC Labor Contract Law provides that after execution of two consecutive fixed-term labor contracts, an employee can request an open-term contract (unless grounds for termination exist). However, as is typical of so much relating to China's employment laws, different places in China have different interpretations. For example, Beijing allows an employer to terminate the employee at the end of the first contract term. But if the employer does not terminate the employee at that time, the contract automatically becomes an open-term contract. This is another reason why we[68] generally advise our employer clients to use an initial employment term of three years and a probation period of six months (the longest probation period possible) for their new employees, because in cities like Beijing, employers get only one shot at fixed-term employment.

In Shanghai, once an employee has completed two fixed-term contracts for an employer, the employee is entitled to an open-ended

---

[68] http://www.harrisbricken.com/

contract. But Shanghai's interpretation is different from Beijing's in that an employer in Shanghai is free to decide not to retain the employee after the second term. Note, however, that the employer's decision to let the employee go is not without monetary obligations: it must pay statutory severance to the employee. Generally, the employer must pay one month's salary for every full year the employee has worked for the employer and half a month's salary for less than six months' service. If the employee has worked for more than six months but less than one year, that employee is treated as if he or she had worked for a full year.

To sum up, employees in China are generally entitled to an open-ended contract, provided each of the following conditions have been met:

1. The employee has completed two consecutive fixed-term contracts (but note how Beijing is different on this).
2. The employer has no statutory grounds for terminating its employee.
3. BOTH parties agree to renew the contract for a third time.
4. The employee requests an open-ended contract.

To repeat, an open-ended term usually will not happen unless both the employer and the employee agree to renew the contract after completion of two terms. Thus, if the employer wants to re-hire the employee but refuses to do so on an open-term basis, the employee will not be able to force the employer to hire him or her on an open-term basis. So in Shanghai, once the employee has completed two fixed-term contracts, the employer has three options:

1. Let the employee go and pay the applicable statutory severance.
2. Enter into an open-term contract with the employee that provides for lifetime employment.
3. Persuade the employee to voluntarily accept a third fixed-term contract.

It is the rare employee who turns down lifetime employment in favor of a fixed-term contract without added monetary incentives.

SIX COMMON MYTHS ABOUT CHINA EMPLOYMENT LAWS

I have been writing a lot lately about various myths regarding specific aspects of Chinese employment law. The below posts set forth many of those myths:

- China Employment Law: Six Myths About China Employee Benefits[69]
- China Employment Law: Six Myths About China Employee Non-Compete Agreements[70]
- China Employment Law: Six Myths About Working Hours and Overtime[71]
- China Employment Law: Six Myths About China Employee Probation[72]

---

[69] http://www.chinalawblog.com/2016/12/china-employment-law-six-myths-about-china-employee-benefits.html
[70] http://www.chinalawblog.com/2016/12/six-myths-about-china-employee-non-compete-agreements.html
[71] http://www.chinalawblog.com/2016/11/china-employment-law-six-myths-about-working-hours-and-overtime.html
[72] http://www.chinalawblog.com/2016/11/six-myths-about-china-employee-probation.html

- China Employment Law: The Myths and the Realities of Employee Severance[73]

But I have yet to write about the most common China employment law myths overall. Until now.

Myth 1: A China employer can hire an independent contractor to avoid having to hire someone as a regular employee and pay all kinds of employee benefits.

Although retaining someone as an independent contractor is not totally impossible, it can only be done under very limited circumstances. First, you need to consider the tasks of the person you are seeking to hire. For example, if you are a software company and this person is expected to work as a software design engineer, you probably need to retain this person as an employee. If your "independent contractor" is being managed according to your rules and regulations and all other company policies, it is very likely that such a person will be deemed an employee for purposes of Chinese labor law. Moreover, if you wish to have full control over this person's behavior, you might as well hire him or her as an employee in the first place. This is not something you want to get wrong, and yet we constantly see foreign companies get this wrong.

Myth 2: In China, employment at-will is possible, provided there is a well-crafted contract in place.

Wrong. China is not an employment-at-will jurisdiction. Nevertheless, China employees can leave pretty much at any time for pretty much any reason so long as they give advance notice (generally speaking, three days' notice during the probation period and 30 days written notice once the probation period has passed). In some Chinese cities (but not in others), with a well-crafted employment contract in both English and Chinese, it is possible to have an at-will arrangement with a non-Chinese employee.

---

[73] http://www.chinalawblog.com/?s=myths

Myth 3: A China employee on an open-term contract cannot be terminated. Ever.

You cannot terminate a lifetime employee without cause just as generally you cannot terminate an employee on a fixed-term contract without cause. Having an open-term contract means the employee has much more leverage when it comes to negotiating a mutual termination and that you will likely need to pay much more to dismiss the employee than to an employee on a fixed-term contract. However, such employee is not untouchable. For example, if he or she has materially breached your rules and regulations, you may have valid grounds to terminate.

Myth 4: Employer rules and regulations are just a formality. I
cannot stress enough the importance of having a set of English *and* Chinese rules and regulations[74] that work for China. If you don't have these, you should get started drafting them NOW.

Myth 5: Overtime rules are not enforced, and I know this because most other employers in my locale don't follow the overtime rules.

Wrong. The general direction in China is toward more enforcement. Furthermore, "foreign" employers are always going to be under closer scrutiny than their Chinese counterparts. Most important, even if the local human resources and social security authorities are not cracking down on illegal practices in your area, this does not mean your employees will not pursue you in labor arbitration for overtime.

Myth 6: We acknowledge our sales people are employees and we give them all social insurance and other employee benefits, but because they get so much in commissions, we don't need to provide them with any base pay. Wrong.

If someone is hired as an employee, the safest route is to pay him or her a monthly base salary. Generally speaking, the absolute minimum is the local minimum wage standard. It usually does not matter that

---

[74] http://www.chinalawblog.com/2016/04/china-employer-rules-and-regulations-and-why-you-must-have-one.html

the employee's average monthly pay is a lot higher than the local minimum. Where there is no base pay each month, the argument that the employee made a ton during the busy season is likely to fail and you will be deemed to have violated minimum wage laws.

SIX MYTHS ABOUT CHINA EMPLOYEE PROBATION

Chinese labor law permits employers to set a probation period[75] to evaluate their employees' suitability and make a (more or less) informed decision about whether to retain an employee for the long term or even for a life-term. Foreign employers are often confused about employee probation in China. The following are six common myths regarding China employee probation.

Myth 1: The employer doesn't have to contribute to the employee's social insurance account until after the employee has completed his or her probation period to the employer's satisfaction.

Your obligation to pay mandatory social insurance starts as soon as the employee begins working for you.

Myth 2: The employer need not sign a written employment agreement with an employee on probation until the end of the probation period.

---

[75] http://www.chinalawblog.com/2016/06/china-employee-probation-periods-set-it-right.html

The probation period is deemed to be part of the employment period, so you must have a written employment contract with all employees, even those on probation. It's preferable to have the signing "ceremony" on an employee's first day, but in no event should you wait beyond 30 days after your employee's commencement date.

Myth 3: The employer can use a simple "probation period contract" instead of a formal employment contract, because who needs the formalities at this stage? Even if this arrangement does not otherwise violate any Chinese labor laws, this idea is usually not practical. You will need a formal employment contract eventually so you might as well have one at the very outset.

Myth 4: The employer can extend for another probation period[76] if it is not sure about whether to retain this employee beyond the probation period.

Be careful here. Some places do not allow for extending the probation period and the employee's written consent does not matter. Some places may allow it but the combined length of the probation period cannot exceed the statutory maximum.

Myth 5: The probation period is an employment-at-will period so the employer can unilaterally terminate an employee on probation without cause.

You can only terminate an employee when one of the statutory conditions for termination is present. You may unilaterally terminate an employee that does not satisfy your conditions of employment without having to pay severance. But you must be able to prove that the employee failed to meet your standards. A well-documented discharge with a detailed explanation for why the employee does not meet your expectations will significantly reduce your risks of later being sued for wrongful termination.

---

[76] http://www.chinalawblog.com/2014/12/china-employee-probation-you-may-have-just-one-shot.html

Myth 6: An employer that lets an employee go before the expiration of his or her probation period can set a new probation period if it decides to hire the employee back.

Setting a new probation period for the same employee runs afoul of the Chinese labor laws. Though China court decisions on this issue are somewhat inconsistent, we nearly always recommend using only one probation period for the same employee.

BOTTOM LINE: do not use employee probation periods unless and until you know the laws.

WATCHING A BIT OF THE SAUSAGE BEING MADE

The Chinese government is increasingly taking its employment laws more seriously (at least with respect to foreign companies doing business in China). Below is an email from one of our China lawyers (who is doing China employment law about half time these days), with all possible identifiers removed or changed. We are sending a version of this email out a lot these days.

***

As noted in previous emails, employment law in China has been in a state of transition over the past few years. Though the relevant laws have not changed all that much, the implementation of those laws has changed quite a lot, and it remains inconsistent throughout the country. Many of the granular issues, like overtime and working hours, are handled on a case-by-case basis by the relevant local labor bureau, which is why it's so important that we contact them and explain the facts of each situation before moving forward.

Over the past few days we have spoken several times with the [Big China City] labor bureau, and, in particular the _____ District office, which is the office that handles applications and approvals for your WFOE's employees. We explained your WFOE's general approach to them, and we got the following clarification from them regarding _____ District's current practice regarding alternative working hours systems:

1. Mr. Zhang's [not real name] job position and salary make him theoretically eligible for the flexible working hours system. Other sales representatives employed by your WFOE (even those in _____) might also be eligible.

2. We spoke with the supervisor of the _____ District labor bureau about the particulars of Mr. Zhang's employment, and he indicated that there was a good chance Mr. Zhang would be approved to work under the flexible hours system.

3. Your WFOE would need to obtain permission from the _____ District labor bureau BEFORE implementing the flexible working hours system.

4. To implement the flexible working hours system, your WFOE would have to submit the following:

- copies of the WFOE's business license and organization code certificate;

- a list of employees working under the flexible working hours system; and

- a summary of the work and rest schedule for such employees.

5. The _____ labor bureau does not have a formal position on whether (or how) travel time would count as "working hours." Their position is that the WFOE's rules and regulations determine this issue, but the company must ensure that each employee's workload is reasonable. The labor bureau declined to elaborate on the definition of "reasonable," other than to say that "it is what a normal person could finish in a normal amount of time" and that "any application for the flexible working hours system would have to explain how each employee's workload was reasonable." This is pretty typical, and we have quite a lot of experience handling this.

6. Your WFOE can prepare and submit this application itself or you can authorize one of our China lawyers to do it on your behalf.

7. Upon receiving an application, the labor bureau will render an initial decision within 5 business days. However, the _____ District

supervisor indicated that much of the time, the bureau will issue a decision on the spot.

8. The labor bureau will subsequently issue a formal decision. Any approval for the flexible hours working system will indicate the term of the approval, which can be for up to two years.

At this point, I suggest that you think about your approach to travel time and working hours for sales representatives and then we should discuss that. Depending on what you decide, we may want to add a line or two to Article _____ of your Rules and Regulations.

CHINA EMPLOYMENT OFFER LETTERS: BE CAREFUL

In China, an offer letter is a written document delivered by an employer to an employee stating the employer's intent to enter into a labor relationship with the employee. An offer letter typically proposes the employee's work title, work location, wages, and the term of the employment arrangement.

Despite the relatively common use of employment offer letters in China (especially by state-owned enterprises) no Chinese law specifically addresses them. For that reason and for the reasons set forth below, employers should be careful when using them.

To begin with, despite what many believe, offer letters are *not* an official labor contract and they do not satisfy the requirement[77] that labor contracts be in writing. Under Chinese law, an offer letter is regarded as an employer's unilateral act expressing its willingness to enter into an employment relationship with a potential employee. An offer letter is deemed to be an "offer" and it is governed by China's Contract Law, not by China's Labor Contract Law. A labor contract is a legal document evidencing the existence of a labor relationship between the employer and the employee, but an offer letter has no

---

[77] http://www.chinalawblog.com/2010/10/china_employment_contracts_dont_ leave_home_without_it.html

such effect. So even when the employee returns a signed offer letter, the employer must nevertheless execute a formal labor contract with the employee within one month after the employee begins working for the employer to be in compliance with Chinese law.

Under China's Labor Contract Law,[78] an employer can be required to pay its employees twice the employees' monthly salary if it fails to execute a written labor contract within one month of the commencement of the employment relationship. Further, if the employer goes more than a year without having a written labor contract with an employee, the employee lacking the written labor contract will be deemed to have entered into an open-term labor contract with its employer, which essentially means there is no definitive end date to the labor relationship.

Nearly all the offer letters our China lawyers have reviewed made statements violating PRC labor laws. This alone generally makes it a bad idea to refer to the offer letter in any eventual labor contract. And on top of this, nearly all the offer letters we see also usually contain terms that **conflict** with the labor contracts and/or other employment agreements such as the employer's rules and regulations.

When an offer letter makes sense for our clients, we usually recommend that they insert a provision in the formal labor contract (in Chinese, of course) explicitly providing that the labor contract supersedes[79] the offer letter.

In conclusion, if you are going to use an offer letter, you should, at minimum, make sure of the following:

- It does not violate any PRC laws.
- You have a written labor contract with the employee to whom you sent the offer letter.
- Your written labor contract clearly provides (in Chinese) that it supersedes the offer letter.

---

[78] http://www.chinalawblog.com/2008/06/chinas_new_labor_contract_law_2.html
[79] http://www.merriam-webster.com/dictionary/supersede

WHEN IN CHINA. . .
CHINA LABOR LAW CONTROLS

Here's an email I recently received from a friend:

I am heading off again to work for a few years at our China Rep Office. My new employment contract with the head office says that [foreign country] law will apply. Will it? And what if there is a conflict between [the foreign country] law and China's laws, which will control?

We get this question far too frequently, and we have seen way too many employment contracts written as though U.S. law (it was actually not a U.S. company in the above instance) applies all around the world. The reality is that if you are working for a Chinese company in China (be it a Rep Office, a WFOE, a JV, or whatever), Chinese law is going to apply to your employment relationship. I know of no country that would allow otherwise. I mean, imagine if a United States subsidiary of a Pakistani company were to claim in a U.S. court that it should not be required to pay overtime because their contract with the employee calls for Pakistani law and Pakistani law does not provide for that, or that it can discriminate against women because there is no such law prohibiting that in Pakistan? Even if the employee at issue were a Pakistani citizen, there is absolutely no way in the world a U.S. court would go along with any of those arguments. In fact, the argument is so bizarre I am not even aware of anyone ever having made it.

Any employer-employee relationship between a Chinese company and an employee working in China is going to be governed by China law, no matter what the contract says. So in China there would be no conflict of laws because Chinese law would simply apply. This is why we also advocate for drafting China employment contracts and employee manuals with Chinese as the official language. Chinese courts and Chinese administrative bodies are the only rightful jurisdiction for China labor law disputes stemming from employment in China (and yes, this is true for expats too) and so it only makes sense to have these documents in the language they are sure to understand.

Here is a more interesting, complicated, and related question: what would happen if a U.S. company had a contract with a U.S. citizen and that contract provided that the U.S. citizen go work at the U.S. company's WFOE for a few years, and that contract called for application of U.S. law? Now, as I have said above, no Chinese court would apply anything but Chinese law to this relationship. But what would happen if the U.S. citizen were to flip around and sue the U.S. company in a U.S. court for failing to abide by some particular U.S. law? I do not know the answer to this question, but I can tell you that if it were to benefit my client, I would argue that Chinese law applies and I **think** I would prevail on that. And I can also tell you that if it were to benefit my client, I would argue that U.S. law applies.

YOUR ONE BAD EXAMPLE DOES NOT A LEGAL SYSTEM MAKE

Here's a really interesting, somewhat angry email I received related to an article published on our China law blog. Please review it along with my response:

> Hi, I'm an American citizen that just got fired in China, and I have to say, you make it sound a lot harder than it actually was. Did Chinese employment law change that much since you wrote the article[80] in 2010?
>
> I worked full time for a very large company in _____[city] legally. I have my foreign expert's certificate, Z-visa, and everything.
>
> NO compensation, NO notice, in spite of the contract stipulating notice was necessary. Just fired this month actually.
>
> I'm not under criminal investigation, nor did I commit any serious dereliction of duty. They apparently got one complaint about me, the "proof" of which they declined to give me.
>
> I know that it's a Chinese company and an American citizen, not an American company/Chinese citizen, but aren't all of these entities bound by Chinese law over here? You didn't cite any sources in this article. Shouldn't any analysis of Chinese law use some kind of

---

[80] http://www.chinalawblog.com/2010/01/terminating_your_china_employe.html

> *primary or even secondary source? I mean I know it's just a blog, but putting spurious stuff up does affect people. Unless I'm wrong. But from my perspective they can "fire an employee for good reason, bad reason, or no reason at all" in China easily.*

My perhaps too blunt response was as follows:

> No they can't. If you sue them and you lose, then let's talk. All you have sent me is what looks like the ten millionth case of a Chinese company taking advantage of a foreign employee it thinks is either too poor, too afraid, or too disconnected from having the ability to just hire a lawyer and sue. Get a lawyer and do something. Do anything. But don't bother complaining to me about your own problems/inaction. Again, if you sue and lose, then we will have something to talk about.

BOTTOM LINE (again): Employers in China must follow a whole host of rules. Just because they often violate those rules does not mean they are not required to follow them. It also does not mean they will get away with violating those rules if sued. I am not telling anyone to sue, but I am saying that it is our experience that the employee in China who actually stands up for his or her rights in China (at least as against foreign companies, which is all that we ever represent) usually prevails.

PERSONAL LIABILITY FOR FAILED CHINA WFOES: THE LAW AND THE REALITY

The economic slowdown in North America and Europe has left many WFOEs in China with insufficient funds to continue their business activities. These WFOEs often have to suddenly shut down, leaving numerous unpaid debts. We have received a number of calls from worried general managers and directors concerning their personal liability in these situations.

I will describe the normal scenario below, followed by the usual questions and the answer under Chinese law.

THE STORY:

1. A WFOE is owned by a U.S. or European shareholder. The WFOE is engaged in small-scale manufacturing. The WFOE has 100 Chinese employees and numerous Chinese suppliers.

2. The WFOE has been in business for three years. The WFOE has never made a profit in China. The shareholder has been required to make repeated cash payments to the WFOE to cover the WFOE's salary and other expenses.

3. The foreign shareholder suffers a financial setback. The foreign shareholder files for bankruptcy, or the shareholder's bank shuts down all loans, or the shareholder's investors refuse to make additional capital contributions to the WFOE. As a result, the shareholder cuts off all funds to the WFOE. The cash flow of the WFOE is not sufficient to cover the requirements of the WFOE.

4. The China-based management of the WFOE is unprepared for the cut off in funds. The WFOE owes:

   - One month or more salary to workers, plus severance owed to workers if their employment is terminated.
   - Debt to suppliers and rent to landlord.
   - Taxes.

   The WFOE will never be able to repay these amounts because it is operating at a substantial loss and its shareholder will no longer cover it.

THE QUESTIONS:

We are then contacted by the China resident general manager/representative director/shareholder of the WFOE with the following questions:

QUESTION: What is the personal liability of the foreign national general manager?

ANSWER: The general manager is simply an employee of the WFOE. A general manger is under no circumstances legally liable for the debts of the WFOE.

———◆———

QUESTION: What is the personal liability of the representative director?

ANSWER: The representative director is not liable for any of the debts of the WFOE either. The answer here is somewhat complex. The official interpretation of the PRC Company Law, issued by the PRC Supreme Court (Articles 18/19), is that a director of a limited liability company is never liable for the debts of a limited liability company. Only the shareholder is liable. But the shareholder is liable only in the case of intentional fraud designed to divert funds to harm creditors. Note that for companies delimited by shares, the directors can be held liable, but only in the case of affirmative fraud. WFOEs are limited liability companies, so this provision does not apply. Note that this relief from liability for directors applies to all directors, without distinction as to whether the director is the legal representative of the WFOE.

————◆————

QUESTION: What is the effect for the general manager, legal representative, or the directors if they want to obtain employment at a different WFOE in China after the failure of the WFOE discussed above? What is the effect if they want to be the director of a different WFOE in China?

ANSWER: Legally, there is no effect. Such persons are free to take up employment in any other organization located in China because, as discussed above, no personal liability of any kind is imposed on these persons.

————◆————

QUESTION: What is the effect for the general manager, legal representative, or the directors if they want to act as shareholders in a different WFOE in China?

ANSWER: There is no effect. However, if the general manager, director, or shareholder have been involved in a bankruptcy where it was determined that the bankruptcy occurred because of their intentional fraudulent actions, such persons will be prevented from acting as a director or general manager for three years.

————◆————

QUESTION: What is the effect for the shareholder of the failed WFOE if it wants to make an investment to form a different WFOE in China? We have been told that such a shareholder will be prevented from making a new investment. Is this true?

ANSWER: There is no legal restriction for a shareholder to form a new WFOE when that shareholder has been an investor in a previously failed WFOE.

———◆———

QUESTION: We have been told that it is a crime to fail to pay the salaries of employees in China and that the general manager and legal representative can be held liable for such a crime. Is this true?

ANSWER: It is a crime for the "responsible persons" in a company to fail to pay workers when funds for such payment are available. It is not a crime to fail to pay workers due to insolvency, as described in the scenario we are discussing.

———◆———

The analysis above is based on China's *written law*. With respect to future employment and future investment, we have not personally encountered this kind of blackballing in China. We have heard a number of stories about this having occurred, but we have not been able to verify any of them.

On the issue of payments to employees and creditors of the WFOE, the situation is more complex. China is a rough place. Out in the real world, there are two problems to consider:

1.   Many local governments do not care about the written law. Local governments are particularly concerned about payment of employees and payment of taxes. Where WFOEs fail and these amounts remain unpaid, the local government will often apply strong pressure on any locally based foreign staff to try to force payment. This can involve various threats of sanctions against the locally based foreign staff, regardless of their status in the WFOE. These threats, though not legally based, should be taken very seriously. For this reason, we recommend that when this kind of

problem occurs, locally based foreign staff leave China (or at least the local area) as quickly as possible. We have had to deal with this sort of situation many times, particularly in third and fourth tier cities.

2. The more serious threat in China is that Chinese creditors fully understand that locally based staff are not liable for the debts of the WFOE. They also understand that as a limited liability company, the shareholder is also not liable for payment of the debts of the WFOE. And they also understand that WFOEs want to protect their staff and the remaining company assets and records. They therefore take matters into their own hands and threaten to, or commit, various violent acts against company staff and company property in an attempt to force payment. This usually involves taking staff hostage or wholesale destruction of company property. In many locations in China, government authorities and police will do little or nothing to prevent such violent acts. Again, for this reason, we recommend that staff leave China (or at least the local area) as soon as possible when it appears that it will be impossible to make payments to employees or local vendors. This kind of situation can get out of hand very quickly in China and this sort of situation is not at all rare, depending in large part on the locale.

BEIJING EMPLOYMENT RULES: TIGHTER AND TIGHTER

In September 2014, the Beijing Human Resources and Social Security Bureau, Foreign Affairs Office of the Beijing Municipality and Beijing Education Commission jointly published the Circular on Further Strengthening the Employment of Foreigners in Beijing ("the Circular"). In this post, I highlight a few key aspects of this Circular.

According to the Circular, foreigners may be employed in Beijing only if they satisfy the following conditions:

1. The candidate is in good health.
2. The candidate does not have any criminal record.
3. The candidate is between the ages of 18 and 60 (subject to the exception noted below).
4. The candidate must possess a valid passport or other valid travel document in lieu of a passport.
5. The candidate must have a specified employer.
6. The candidate must have a bachelor's degree or higher and possess a minimum of two years' work experience in the relevant area, with the exception of language teachers, who must have at least five years of work experience in the relevant field. However, for senior technicians urgently needed for tasks relating to key technology or research and development, a candidate without a bachelor's degree can be employed upon

providing a certificate proving the relevant skills or qualifications.

7. The candidate must obtain a work permit and a residence permit for work purposes and cannot take on any job beyond the permitted scope of the work permit.

The circular also provides that the age and work experience requirements are not absolute, and to the extent certain talents are "immediately needed" in Beijing, these requirements may be relaxed. The Circular does not define what would qualify as "immediately needed talents" and the Beijing Labor Bureau has not issued any written guidelines on this. We would expect that the more specialized or rare the skills, the more likely the admittance.

Additionally, the Beijing employer is required to enter into a written labor contract with the foreign employee, the term of which cannot exceed five years but may be renewed indefinitely. The Circular also reinforces the requirement that the employer contribute to social insurance for the non-Chinese employee. Employers that fail to pay the full amount of social insurance may be subjected to an administrative fine up to three times the outstanding amount. The Circular also mandates that employers maintain a copy of the following employment-related documents: the labor contract, a copy of the employee's passport, a copy of the employee's work certificate, a copy of the employee's temporary residence registration form, proof of the employee's lack of criminal history abroad (I note how much fun it is proving that someone does not have a criminal record!), the employee's attendance records, the records of social insurance payments on behalf of the employee, and the employee's wage payment history.

The employer must apply for cancellation of the employee's work permit within 10 days after termination of the employee's labor contract. If the employer wishes to renew its employee's labor contract, it must do so by submitting an application with the relevant authorities at least 60 days before the expiration of the employee's work permit, otherwise the non-Chinese employee's work permit expires immediately upon expiration of the term of the labor contract.

BOTTOM LINE: Beijing is very serious about the applicable employment laws and rules and we strongly advise our clients that compliance will, in the long term, be cheaper than non-compliance. If you are an employer in Beijing, you need to be mindful of the requirements imposed by this Circular in addition to the relevant national regulation and local rules.

CHINA EMPLOYMENT LAW: LOCAL AND NOT SO SIMPLE

Recently, I had the chance to write a Forbes Magazine article (China's Hourly Work Week: Think Locally[81]) emphasizing how China's employment laws are so localized. I started that article with the following explanation:

> *I have avoided writing on China employment law because it is so complicated and so localized. My fear has been that any single article can only scratch the surface.*

Bearing that thesis in mind, let's touch on something that should be pretty simple: the hourly work week.

Every December, our China lawyers receive at least quadruple the usual number of emails relating to China employment issues. This time of year we get a slew of emails from companies doing business in China with questions about their employees and an even greater number of emails from employees with questions about their employment situation, usually involving their wanting to move on to a different employer.

---

[81] http://www.forbes.com/sites/danharris/2015/01/27/chinas-hourly-workweek-think-locally/

The employees often want us to give them a quick (and free) answer to their questions, not realizing how complicated they really are.

Here is an example of typical email we receive from employees, with changes made to hide any identifiers:

> *I am a long time reader of your blog and I now finally need your help. I work for a US WOFE, residence permit, paying taxes, everything is right. Some time ago, a _____ company asked me to collaborate as a volunteer for them one day a week. I am really interested in this company and what they do and so I have the following quick questions for you. Would it be a legal problem if I do this once a week volunteering? Do I need a certificate or document saying that I am working with them because I want to help people and at the same time do _____? Do I need approval from my existing employer to do this extra work? They also tell me that maybe in the future they can give me some money for the collaboration. Again, would that be a problem with my current job?*

Our quick answer to this email is indicative of how we usually respond:

> *Our short answer is that we don't know the answers to your questions and we cannot even begin to help you unless and until we know who your employer is and can run a conflict check on that company. I urge you to search out our blog articles on China employment law because if you do you will understand why we cannot give quick answers here. China's employment laws and regulations vary from city to city and they depend on the specific situation. For us to be able to give you anything resembling actionable advice we would need to know ALL the facts of your situation, especially the city (or cities) you are discussing, then review the contract you have with your employer and then research the applicable laws and regulations in the relevant city (or cities) and then discuss these laws and regulations with the appropriate governmental authorities. We'd be happy to represent you (if we can), but you will need to decide whether paying legal fees makes sense for you. I suggest you reach out to a local Chinese lawyer for this.*

Not sure why, but we by far get more requests (by a wide margin) for answers to "quick" or "simple" questions relating to China labor law than to any other legal issue. I have written this post to try to spread the word that there are very few routine answers when it comes to Chinese employment law.

CHINA EMPLOYMENT LAW: THE MYTHS AND THE REALITIES OF EMPLOYEE SEVERANCE

Generally speaking, once an employee has completed his or her probation period, termination[82] requires severance payment. Note also that even when the employer and the employee *mutually* decide to terminate their employment relationship, a severance payment is usually required if the employer is the one that initiated the conversation about ending the employment relationship.

Under the PRC Labor Contract Law, the amount of severance that must be paid to the employee is based primarily on the employee's wages and years of employment. The law provides that for each year (which is any period longer than six months) the employee has worked for the employer, the employee will be entitled to one month's wages. For any period of employment of less than six months, the employee will be entitled to half a month's wages. So for example, if your employee worked for you for 30 years and four months, you must pay 30.5 months of his or her wages as severance payment.

---

[82] http://www.chinalawblog.com/2015/04/terminating-china-employees-the-basics.html

However, as one of my favorite law professors at Beida[83] used to say: in your practice, you will find a general rule on a particular issue and then you will find an exception to the basic rule and then you will find an exception to that exception. One exception to the basic rule above is that if your employee's monthly wage exceeds 300% of the local average monthly wage, then the latter should be used in calculating his or her severance payment. Here is an additional wrinkle: in this situation, the number of years of service used to calculate statutory severance will be capped at 12 years.

But this is not the end of the story. For example, things can get even more complicated when you are dealing with an employee who started working for you before the current PRC Labor Contract Law came into effect on January 1, 2008. Suppose you are terminating an employee whose monthly wage during the last 12 months of employment is higher than 300% of the local average monthly wage. Because the Labor Contract Law does not operate retroactively on this, the employee's years of employment before 2008 will not be subject to the 300%-local-average-monthly-wage cap and thus the employee's actual monthly wage should be used for those years. The years of employment after 2008, however, will be subject to the 300% cap.

As is true of nearly everything related to China employment law,[84] the application of what is a relatively clear national law can vary on the local level. For example, some municipalities apply a 12-month cap under a wider range of circumstances than the national rule. And in Shanghai, if the employee is forced to unilaterally terminate the employment contract due to the employer's fault (e.g., violence or threats by the employer), the statutory severance will also be subject to a 12-month cap.

At the end of an initial employment term, if an employer does not wish to extend the contract to its employee, it must pay severance. Furthermore, if the employee quits because of employer abuse (*e.g.*, failure to pay the employee wages on time per the employment contract), the employer must pay statutory severance to the employee

---

[83] https://en.wikipedia.org/wiki/Peking_University

[84] http://www.chinalawblog.com/2015/12/china-employment-law-local-and-not-so-simple.html

as well. And don't forget that the employer is required to withhold any applicable individual income tax on the severance payment.

CHINA EMPLOYMENT ARBITRATION: GOOD LUCK WITH THAT BATTLE

Every few weeks one of our China lawyers will get an email from a foreign company (virtually always a WFOE) that is in a dispute with its China employee. They usually are surprised that they are in the dispute because they are of the view that they did nothing wrong. Too often they believe that hiring us will involve our spending an hour or two reviewing the facts and the law, and then telling them they did nothing wrong, and then making the case go away.

It most emphatically does not work that way. In fact, in almost all instances when we are brought on to help a foreign company involved in an employee dispute, our advice is to reach an agreement with the employee and then memorialize that agreement with a Chinese language settlement agreement that will make sure there will be no future problems with that employee.

I was cc'ed on an email recently that describes how difficult and expensive these cases can be. The email stated:

I think it important I be upfront on how we view China employment arbitration cases. We view them as typically unwinnable and nearly always not worth the money to fight.

Take your Qingdao matter. For us to sort through all of the factual and legal issues could end up costing you $10,000. And once we sort through all of them, the odds are good that the best we can tell you is that you have some chance to prevail on a few of them, virtually no chance to prevail on most of them, and absolutely no chance to prevail on some of them. Employers only very seldom win against their China employees, foreign employers even less so. And with the recent downturn in China's economy, the odds for employers have gotten even worse. And if you did anything wrong in shutting down your office (and the odds are good that you did), your chances will be even lower.

And then there is the cost of preparing for the arbitration and arbitrating.

So what we suggest our clients do in these situations is try to settle these cases, with all employees. And we have never not succeeded in settling such cases, usually for about half of what the employee was originally seeking. Generally, Chinese employees want quick money and want to get on with their lives, believing that they can get another job (and often already have). The down economy may impact this thinking somewhat, but interestingly enough, past downturns have really not. So if you were to retain us, the first thing we would do is some quick research on the issues. Not anything approaching the $10,000 worth of research necessary to make arguments to an arbitration panel, but just enough to be able to have a really good idea of the employees' weak points that we can highlight in settlement talks. And then we work to settle, and when we settle we document the settlement in such a way as to ensure that the employees do not return.

We would also want to look into the issues with your other employees at your other locations to try to nip potential problems there in the bud. The earlier you can resolve these sorts of issues with employees the better. We have handled a number of office closings, including in Qingdao, and we like to settle with the employees before the closing even happens, when they have a few more months even to work and are feeling safe. I assume we are too late to do that here with your _____ office, but the sooner we deal with the other employees, the less this is all going to cost you.

If you agree with the above approach, we should talk some more. If you do not, well then you should not retain us. Either way, I wish you the best with this difficult situation.

CHINA EMPLOYMENT LAW:
A SEXUAL HARASSMENT CASE STUDY

On our blog, I previously[85] wrote how an employer would be required to pay statutory severance to an employee who unilaterally terminated his or her employment contract because of employer abuse. One such ground is the employer's failure to provide necessary labor protections for employees. For example, China's Law on the Protection of Women's Rights and Interests explicitly prohibits sexual harassment against women, and the law further provides that female sexual harassment victims may file a complaint with their employer and/or with the authorities. Nevertheless, not all female employees have prevailed in getting their employer to pay.

Let's take a look at a case from Zhejiang province.

Employee (plaintiff) entered an employment contract with her employer (defendant) and thus established an employment relationship with the employer in December 2011. In May 2014, the employee found some strange fluid in her mug on her desk and suspected it was semen. She reported this to her employer. The employer contacted the police department and pulled surveillance

---

[85] http://www.chinalawblog.com/2016/05/china-employment-law-statutory-severance.html

video. The next day, the plaintiff/employee took the surveillance video and the mug to the local police. That same day, a male company manager who worked in the same department as the suspect asked the employee who had found the mug on her desk not to press charges against the suspect so that he wouldn't lose face. The following day, the suspect went to the police and confessed everything. The police administratively detained the suspect for three days as punishment, but brought no criminal charges against him.

The following month, the female employee provided notice to her employer of her intention to terminate the employment contract due to the employer's failure to provide labor protection and labor conditions required under the law. The employee demanded three months' statutory severance, but the employer refused to pay. The employee filed a claim against the employer at the labor arbitration center, but she lost. She then filed a lawsuit against the employer in the local court.

The court first acknowledged that the Special Rules on the Labor Protection of Female Employees and other relevant laws and regulations regarding protection of women's rights require an employer to prevent and stop sexual harassment against female employees. But the court then went on to say this does not make employers strictly liable[86] for every illegal act that occurs at the employer's workplace. The court then ruled that even though the suspect was an employee of the defendant, the suspect committed the illegal act himself, and it was his act that directly and proximately caused the employee's emotional stress, which led to her leaving the employment. According to the court, the suspect had acted completely on his own, and the employer had no way of predicting and controlling the suspect's action. After the employer received the employee's report, it handled the incident as best as it could by timely contacting the police and pulling the surveillance video. The court went on to hold that the department manager who asked the female employee to withdraw her complaint about the incident was not representing the employer with that request and thus his actions also did not constitute employer action. Finally, after the police had punished the suspect, the employer terminated him. So there was no factual or legal basis to support the employee's demand for severance when she unilaterally

---

[86] https://en.wikipedia.org/wiki/Strict_liability

terminated the employment relationship with the employer. Thus the employee lost at the court level as well.

How would a U.S. court have handled this same case? To get an answer to this, I turned to my friend, Ada Wong,[87] a Seattle-based employment attorney licensed in the states of Washington and California. She surprisingly responded by saying that a Washington State Court would probably have handled the case quite similarly:

In Washington, employers also have a duty to prevent workplace harassment, including sexual harassment. However, employers are not automatically held liable for every employee's actions. Under federal law, an employer is subject to vicarious liability to employees for an actionable hostile work environment created by a supervisor. It is unclear from the facts of this case whether the suspect/perpetrator would be considered a "supervisor" so as to render the employer strictly liable for that person's actions. If the perpetrator had held the power to hire, fire, demote, fail to promote, etc., then that person would likely have been considered a supervisor for this purpose.

If the employer had reason to know – "knew or should have known" – that the perpetrator was engaging in this type of behavior or was going to engage in this type of behavior, and still failed to prevent it, then the employer could be held liable for allowing the perpetrator to carry out his actions.

The employer took the correct action by immediately reporting it to the police and starting an investigation by pulling the surveillance video.

In terms of the department manager who requested that the harassed employee withdraw her complaint, it is unclear whether he represented the employer when he made that request. If he did this while at the office during working hours, then plaintiff could argue that she was under the impression that if she did not withdraw her complaint, she could face adverse employment action. Had she reported this to her employer and was terminated or faced adverse employment action, that would have provided her with additional grounds for a lawsuit. The department manager's telling the plaintiff/employee not to press charges was clearly inappropriate, but it may not give rise to a claim against the employer.

---

[87] http://www.akwlawpllc.com/#%21people/cjg9

If this matter were heard in a Washington state court and there had been no evidence of any prior notice of the suspect's inappropriate behavior, the plaintiff employee likely would not prevail on a sexual harassment claim against her employer for the suspect's action, especially because the employer took appropriate measures, including contacting the police and terminating the suspect upon learning of the incident. If plaintiff employee could show that the department manager was acting in his supervisory capacity when he requested that she withdraw her complaint, then the employer may be deemed liable.

This case is unusual in that the suspect's action was so bizarre that it is hard to imagine the employer could or should have foreseen it. Still, the Chinese court never even discussed the "notice" element: did the employer have reason to know (or even have an inkling) that the perpetrator would do something like this?

What is also unusual about this case is that the employer chose to spend money fighting this battle in a court and thereby allowing all of this to become public, rather than just paying the employee her three months.

CHINA EMPLOYMENT LAWS: GET THEM RIGHT OR FACE PUBLIC CONSEQUENCES

The PRC Ministry of Human Resources and Social Security recently released a set of rules on providing public notice of China employer labor violations (重大劳动保障违法行为社会公布办法). The goal of these new rules is obvious: it is intended to deter employers from violating China's labor and employment laws and regulations. These rules went into effect on January 1, 2017 and apply to all China employers, *domestic and foreign*. The following rulings/decisions on employer violations of China's labor laws may become public:

- failing to pay "substantial" employee remuneration;
- failing to pay an employee's social insurance[88] and the circumstances are "serious";
- violating the laws on working time, rest, or vacation[89] and the circumstances are "serious";
- violating the special rules on protecting female workers and underage workers and the circumstances are "serious";

---

[88] http://www.chinalawblog.com/2016/09/eight-keys-for-navigating-chinas-employment-laws.html

[89] http://www.chinalawblog.com/2016/02/china-employee-vacation-law.html

- violating the child labor laws;
- causing significantly bad social consequences due to violations of labor laws; or
- other serious illegal conduct.

Neither "substantial" nor "serious" are anywhere defined.

When publishing these labor law decisions, the following information will be released to the public (with exceptions for national security, trade secrets, or individual privacy):

- the employer's full name, integrated social credit code/registration number, and address;
- the name of the legal representative or the person-in-charge;
- the main facts of the violation; and
- the decision made by the authorities.

The above information will be published on the labor authorities' portal as well as in major newspapers, magazines, TV, and other media each quarter at the city/county level and twice a year at the provincial and national level. This information will go into the employer's credit file on integrity and legal compliance and may be shared with other governmental departments. The employer can file a petition with the relevant labor authorities if it does not agree with what has been published, and the authorities will render a decision within 15 working days and notify the employer. If the published information has been modified or withdrawn according to law, the relevant authorities will modify the published content within 10 working days.

The rules are not very detailed, which comes as no surprise. China's local human resources and social security bureaus will be responsible for implementing these rules and they presumably will have considerable discretion about how they do so. Note, however, that they don't get to cherry pick what to publish: if a violation meets the applicable standard, it will be published.

As of January 1, 2017, if a China employer commits a serious violation of Chinese labor and employment laws, it may be made public by the labor authorities. Make sure you are in compliance and that you stay in compliance.[90] And if you do not know whether you are in compliance, figure it out. NOW.

To say we are concerned for our clients for whom we do not conduct regular employer/employee audits is an **understatement**. It is getting progressively more difficult for foreign companies doing business in China to compete with domestic companies in hiring Chinese workers. And a foreign company that gets publicly excoriated for employer misconduct will no doubt find it even more difficult and expensive to find good workers. We see far too many foreign companies doing business in China with little or no clue about its employment laws. Some still believe China today is the same as China a decade ago, where unhappy employees could be bought off with a month or two of wages because they knew they could (and they did) easily move on to another job.

Those days are over and we fear foreign employers will be disproportionately singled out for public approbation.

As we have been pointing out pretty much since we started this blog, going after foreign companies in China is simply good politics. It always has been and always will be. Read Machiavelli.[91] Read Sun Tzu.[92] Read Animal Farm.[93] Read 1984.[94] Just look at what pretty much every country in the world does.

And going after foreigners inevitably picks up during economic slowdowns, for generally political reasons. Just look at the U.S. election.

---

[90] http://www.chinalawblog.com/2016/08/china-compliance-a-basic-checklist.html

[91] http://www.bloomberg.com/news/2013-07-17/machiavelli-s-political-survival-guide-gets-french-update.html

[92] http://socialmediatoday.com/index.php?q=cpollittiu/1572221/10-executive-marketing-lessons-sun-tzu-s-art-war

[93] http://www.amazon.com/gp/product/0451526341/ref=as_li_ss_tl?ie=UTF8&camp=1789&creative=390957&creativeASIN=0451526341&linkCode=as2&tag=chinalawblogc-20

[94] http://www.sparknotes.com/lit/1984/

Many years ago, in a Wall Street Journal op-ed entitled, "China's Slowdown and You,"[95] Dan Harris, one of the China lawyers at my firm,[96] asserted, among other things, the following on doing business in China during a slowdown:

- The Chinese government "is much more concerned with social harmony than with economic numbers" and that is why it is continuing to encourage wage growth even though higher wages make China's factories less competitive.

- China's prioritization of its citizens' contentment means China is going to get tougher on foreigners, just as it (and nearly every other country) has always done when times are tough. Everything foreign businesses do will be under heightened scrutiny.

- The key to weathering China's slowdown will be for foreign companies to go back to basics: think afresh about what your company contributes to China's economy and how that is likely to shape policy makers' opinions; focus on scrupulous regulatory compliance; and renew focus on due diligence at a company-to-company level.

Way back in 2006, in a post entitled, ***URGENT ALERT: Register Your Company In China NOW***,[97] we issued our first "urgent alert," noting a crackdown on unregistered companies doing business in China and stressing how foreign companies are never going to be treated like domestic companies:

Long ago, my law firm wrote an article entitled, "Four Essential Principles of Emerging Market Success,"[98] positing that a failure to abide by the law in the country in which you do business is the surest way to lose your business without any basis for complaint.

In many emerging market countries, local businesses take advantage of corruption to avoid complying with laws. This may work for the locals, but it won't work for you. The easiest way for a local rival to

---

[95] http://online.wsj.com/article/SB100008723963904438194045776326835821 98946.html
[96] http://harrisbricken.com/
[97] http://www.chinalawblog.com/2006/11/urgent_alert_register_your_com.html
[98] http://harrisbricken.com/blog/fouressentialprinciples/

drive you out is for you to do something illegal. Neither you nor your government will have good grounds to complain if your rival gets your business closed down because of your illegal activity. It might even be your own partner who reports you so he can assume full ownership and control of your business.

The strength of our views on this has only increased over time. My firm has been contacted far too many times by companies driven out of countries for having engaged in illegal conduct no different from thousands of other foreign companies in the same country. These companies assume they have legal redress, but in reality they almost never do. So long as the law of the country in which the company was operating allows for closures and/or penalties (and in every such situation my firm has encountered, it has), the company is essentially out of luck.

There was a time where most foreign business was illegal in China, particularly as a Wholly Foreign Owned Enterprise (WFOE). Those days are pretty much over now, and the Chinese government knows it. If you came into China as a representative office (rep office) back when that was the only way, and your "registered office" is engaged in business activities that are improper for such an office, the time is now to get that right also.

If your local people in China are telling you this is not how Chinese business is conducted, you need to remind them you are not Chinese and the government will treat you differently. Also remember that your employees' knowledge that you are operating illegally in China gives them tremendous leverage.

Then in 2007, we wrote about this same disparate treatment issue in the context of China's environmental laws in a post entitled, "China Warns Foreign Companies On Pollution"[99]:

China has always and will always (at least for the foreseeable future) enforce its laws more strictly against foreign companies than against domestic companies. I am constantly writing about this not to complain about it, but simply to point out the reality. Just because

---

[99] http://www.chinalawblog.com/2007/10/china_warns_foreign_companies.html

your Chinese domestic competitors are getting away with something does not in any way mean you will be allowed to do so.

Beijing is also now at the stage where it is pretty much neutral about all but the largest foreign companies remaining in China. I am not saying it is neutral about foreign direct investment (FDI) in general, but I am saying that it really could not care less about whether your individual business stays in China or goes. And if your business is a polluter, it actually would probably rather see you leave.

Last, going after foreign companies is politically popular.

We ended that post with the following:

Bottom Line: obey the law, particularly the environmental laws. It is good business.

Certainly the same is now true with respect to China's employment laws.

Similarly, in China Fines Unilever For Mentioning Price Increase. What That Means For YOU,[100] we noted how foreign companies doing business in China cannot expect to be treated like Chinese domestic companies:

As long time readers of our blog know, one of our consistent themes has always been that foreign companies in China should not expect to be treated the same as Chinese domestic companies are, no matter what the laws may say. The reality (not just in China) is that it is usually good politics to go after foreign companies, and it is usually bad politics to go after domestic companies. The reality is also that when a large number of citizens have a particular problem, it is very good politics for the government to show that it is trying to solve it.

Don't end up on social media for violating Chinese labor laws: the costs will be high. Just get it right!

---

[100] http://www.chinalawblog.com/2011/05/china_fines_unilever_for_
mentioning_price_increase_what_that_means_for_you.html

CHINA EMPLOYERS: ARE YOU READY FOR JANUARY 1'S BIG CHANGES?

Earlier this year, the PRC Ministry of Human Resources and Social Security ("MOHRSS") issued a set of Measures for Evaluating Compliance and Integrity of Employers' Labor Protection (企业劳动保障守法诚信等级评价办法). **These Measures took effect on January 1, 2017 and apply to all China employers, domestic and foreign.** So, if you have employees in China and you have not already done so, **NOW** is the time to ask yourself: do you feel ready?

Under these new measures *all* employers in China will be evaluated annually, and based on their legal compliance and any violation, they will be divided into three categories: A, B and C, with C being the lowest category. In conducting its evaluations, the relevant human resources and social authorities will consider each of the following:

- whether the employer has formulated its internal labor protection rules and regulations;[101]
- whether the employer has executed employment contracts[102] with every employee;

---

[101] http://www.chinalawblog.com/2016/04/china-employer-rules-and-regulations-and-why-you-must-have-one.html

- whether the employer is in compliance with labor dispatch laws;
- whether the employer is in violation of the child labor laws;
- whether the employer is in compliance with laws regarding female workers and underage workers;
- whether the employer is in compliance with laws on working hours,[103] rest time, and leave;[104]
- whether the employer is in compliance with laws regarding employee remuneration and meets the applicable minimum wage standard;
- whether the employer contributes all mandatory social insurance; and
- whether the employer is otherwise in compliance with labor protection laws and regulations.

For employers in Category A, the frequency of administrative checks by the local labor authorities will be reduced, while the frequency of inspections for employers in Category B will be increased appropriately (whatever that means), and employers in Category C will become subject to the most scrutiny. Also for employers in Category C, the person-in-charge will be required to schedule meetings with labor authorities to be reminded of the importance of following labor protection laws. The evaluation results will be kept on file for a minimum of three years. You do not want to find yourself in Category C, or even B!

MOHRSS' Measures of Public Disclosure of Significant Violations of Labor Protection Laws (重大劳动保障违法行为社会公布办法) also became effective on January 1, 2017. As discussed in detail above, under these Measures, if a China employer commits a serious violation

---

[102] http://www.chinalawblog.com/2016/04/china-employment-contracts-ten-things-to-consider.html

[103] http://www.chinalawblog.com/2016/11/china-employment-law-six-myths-about-working-hours-and-overtime.html

[104] http://www.chinalawblog.com/2016/10/maternity-leave-in-beijing-its-local-and-its-complicated.html

of Chinese labor and employment laws, it may be made public[105] by the labor authorities.

---

[105] http://www.chinalawblog.com/2016/10/chinas-employment-laws-get-them-right-or-face-very-public-consequences.html

BOTTOM LINE: Effective on the first day of January 2017, two important sets of MOHRSS rules aim to deter employers from violating China's labor and employment laws and regulations. Go ahead and call these legal changes the "China employment lawyers full employment act" (as a couple of our clients already have), but just make sure you are in compliance and you stay in compliance,[106] NOW.

---

[106] http://www.chinalawblog.com/2016/08/china-compliance-a-basic-checklist.html

CHINA EMPLOYERS: PAY YOUR EMPLOYEES ON TIME TO AVOID LAWSUITS AND PENALTIES

As I have previously written, a China employer must pay its employee statutory severance if that employee resigned because of the employer's failure to pay his or her compensation on time or in full. For example, when an employer owes an employee three months' salary, it is likely that the employee can unilaterally terminate the employment relationship and demand all unpaid salary owed to him or her. What constitutes "on time payment" can often be tricky.

Note that in most places in China, employers must pay their employees at least once every month. One question I am often asked is what happens when the employer and the employee contractually agree on a longer payment cycle? In those circumstances, can the employee quit and get statutory severance? The short answer is: usually, yes. Let's take a look at an actual recent case in Shenzhen.

In this case, the employer and employee entered into an employment contract explicitly stating that the employer would pay the employee on the 20th of each month for the previous month's services. The employer was never late in making payment as per the terms of this contract and the employee never objected to the payment terms. But after working for the employer for a while, the employee quit his job and sued the employer for having failed to timely pay him. The company asserted two defenses to the employee's claims: (1) the principle of freedom of contract should apply and the parties' written arrangement on the payment cycle should be upheld; and (2) many employers have financial troubles and pay their employees late, and making employers strictly comply with this employee payment law would be unduly harsh for China employers.

The Shenzhen court found against the employer and for the employee.

The court cited the applicable employee payment regulations in Shenzhen, which essentially require pay dates be no later than seven days after any agreed payment cycle. In other words, an employee must be paid no later than by the seventh day following the month in which he or she provided the service. And if for some reason the employer is unable to pay by the agreed payment date, it may extend that date for up to five days. If after that, the employer is still having financial difficulties, it must obtain written consent from either the labor union or the employee to extend the payment date even further, but in no event may the employer be more than 15 days late in paying.

The court went on to say that even though the regulations allow an employer to make late payment under certain circumstances, this is a very specific exception to the general rule and the employer in this case violated the law by routinely paying late without justification and without following the rules for late payment. Because the employer violated the late payment law, the employee's termination was caused by the employer's failure to compensate him on time. The employee was therefore entitled to tens of thousands of RMB in statutory severance — an amount based on the employee's total years of service for the employer and on his monthly salary.

The employer in this case probably never thought it would have to pay this money because it performed its obligations pursuant to the terms of its contract with its employee.

There is much to be learned from this case about China employment law, including the following:

- It pays to have a qualified lawyer conduct an HR audit[107] of your company and to have this done before your employment problems arise. I would estimate that at least 80 percent of the China employment problems for which my law firm is retained involve issues we easily would have spotted with a simple and relatively inexpensive HR audit. But instead of a relatively leisurely and inexpensive audit, we are instead confronting an angry employee (and often employees) who is threatening to sue or has already sued. One of the first things our China employment lawyers do on a China HR audit is to review our clients' employment contracts and the employer rules and regulations[108] to make sure what is in those critical documents actually accords with all applicable laws, including most importantly, the local laws.

- Timely pay your employees and in full. To do this, you need to know what your local jurisdiction means by "timely."

- Many China employment laws cannot simply be contracted away. It is important that you know what can be changed by contract and what cannot be, and it is important that you also realize all of this can vary depending on where you are and even depending on the type of employee with which you as the employer are contracting. Just by way of a quick example, you will generally have more flexibility in contracting with a COO you are paying USD $40,000 a month than with a factory worker you are paying less than USD $40,000 a year.

- And just to throw in one more point based on an employment matter I recently handled: just because other employers (especially Chinese employers) get away with it does not mean you will too.[109]

---

[107] http://www.chinalawblog.com/2016/11/china-employer-year-end-review-check-these-nine-things-off-your-list.html

[108] http://www.chinalawblog.com/2016/04/china-employer-rules-and-regulations-and-why-you-must-have-one.html

[109] http://www.chinalawblog.com/2017/01/the-six-most-common-myths-about-china-employment-laws.html

- If anything, China gets tougher on employers every year and that — unfortunately — is even more true of foreign companies doing business in China.

Section Three

Frequently Asked Questions about China Labor Law

Regard your soldiers as your children, and they will follow you into the deepest valleys; look on them as your own beloved sons, and they will stand by you even unto death.

~ Sun Tzu

What Do You Need to Know About China Employee Vacation Law?

U nder Chinese labor laws, employees who have worked continuously for one year are entitled to paid annual leave (年休假). The statutory vacation period, based on years of service, is as follows:

- More than 1 and less than 10 years' service: 5 days' vacation.
- More than 10 and less than 20 years' service: 10 days' vacation.
- More than 20 years' service: 15 days' vacation.

"Years of service" is the employee's total years of employment with anyone. This means your new employees may be entitled to paid annual leave during their first year of employment with you as well. The number of paid vacation days your new employee is entitled to is calculated using the following formula: (the remaining calendar days during the calendar year the employee started his/her employment ÷ 365) × the number of statutory vacation days the employee is entitled to under the law (as stated above, this depends on the total number of years the employee has worked).

If you offer more vacation time than the statutory minimum — usually by specifying the more generous vacation time in your rules and regulations — you are legally mandated to provide the extra vacation time you offered.

However, under the following circumstances, the employee is *not* entitled to his or her annual vacation time in the current year:

- the employee has taken summer and winter breaks longer than the statutory annual leave;
- the employee has taken personal leave in excess of 20 days;
- an employee with more than 1 and less than 10 years' service has taken more than 2 months of sick leave;
- an employee with more than 10 and less than 20 years' service has taken more than 3 months of sick leave;
- an employee with more than 20 years' service has taken more than 4 months of sick leave.

Employers are required to make arrangements for employees to take vacation time each year. Unused vacation time in one year may be carried over to the next year, but not beyond that one year. An employer who fails to allow an employee to take annual leave must pay that employee 300% of the employee's daily wages for each unused vacation day. This 300% payment is not required if the employee voluntarily chooses not to take his or her vacation days. However, employers should proceed with caution regarding employees who "volunteer" not to take vacation time because if an employee claims compensation for unused vacation time and the employer cannot produce evidence that the employee voluntarily gave up the unused vacation days, the employer must pay the 300%.

We are aware of many instances where foreign companies were *not* aware of this rule and ended up having to pay a lot of money to Chinese employees who *were*. We advise our clients to make sure that each of their employees take ALL their vacation days or (if this simply is not possible) have employees who are not going to use all their vacation time sign a document in Chinese making very clear it was the employee's own decision to forsake vacation time.

BOTTOM LINE: Chinese labor laws mandate employers arrange for their employees to take paid annual leave and you should think long and hard before you take any of this vacation time away, either by unilateral action or even by agreement.

WHAT HAPPENS TO STUDENT INTERNS IN CHINA?

U ber has recently been getting a lot of media flak for the way it uses interns in China.[110] Hiring interns (like so much else having to do with China employment laws) is complicated and local. And when I am tasked with figuring out how one of our clients may legally do that, I almost always have to review applicable national, provincial, and local laws and regulations and engage in follow-up conversations with the relevant authorities. Not only are there multiple legal layers involved in hiring an intern in China, but those layers are often inconsistent. This is nothing unusual for China employment law. See China Employment Law: It's Complicated and it's Localized.[111]

A domestic or a foreign company in China may not legally "employ" student interns, and student interns that "work" for a company in China are not in a labor relationship under China's labor laws. China's Labor Contract Law is silent on how student interns should be treated. However, this does not mean a Chinese company can or should retain student interns without written documentation. For example, in

---

[110] http://www.ministryoftofu.com/2015/12/uber-accused-of-running-a-sweatshop-of-interns-in-china/

[111] http://abovethelaw.com/2015/01/china-employment-law-its-complicated-and-its-localized/

Jiangsu Province, any company that wants a student intern must execute a formal written agreement with the student intern's school.

There are no hard and fast rules regarding the format of this agreement, but when drafting these for Jiangsu Province, we include the following:

- the term/duration of the internships;
- the responsibilities of the employer;
- the responsibilities of the school;
- the hours and shifts of the internship;
- the intern's compensation;
- applicable provisions on labor protection; and
- applicable provisions addressing accidents, injury, and death.

Just by way of a quick contrast, in Ningbo, a three-party internship agreement is required between the hiring company, the school, and the student or the student's parents.

Another important issue is compensation. In Jiangsu, all interns must be paid directly by the company and such payments must conform to local minimum wage requirements. In Shanghai and Ningbo, however, the minimum compensation payable to student interns is lower than the standard local minimum wage (or at least it was when I researched these cities for a client a few months ago). Ningbo specifically requires that student interns who continuously work for a company for three months or more be paid at least 50% of the preceding year's local minimum wage.

The number of hours an intern can work each day and each week are also all across the board. For example, student interns in Ningbo should work no more than eight hours a day, whereas Jiangsu Province regulations generally limit interns to six hours a day and 30 hours a week, with at least two days off each week.

BOTTOM LINE: though the rules concerning student interns can vary greatly from city to city and province to province, what is consistent between nearly all of them is that they will not tolerate foreign companies using student interns as free labor, especially when labor protections are ignored. If you are using student interns or are contemplating doing so, make it your New Year's resolution to do it correctly.

HOW SHOULD YOU DEAL WITH PREGNANT AND NURSING EMPLOYEES?

How to deal with pregnant or nursing employees has to be one of the most frequently asked questions we get from China employers. The most important thing to know is that Chinese labor law prohibits employers from unilaterally terminating a pregnant or nursing employee.

Many believe you can terminate any China employee, including a pregnant or nursing employee, simply by paying one month's salary for every year the employee has worked for the company. This is *not* true. Termination *without cause* constitutes unlawful termination and will lead to adverse consequences for the employer. Another myth is that you can never terminate a pregnant or nursing employee. An employer can terminate a pregnant or nursing employee without having to pay severance for the employee's material breach of the employer's rules and regulations. [112] However, the rules and regulations provision you use to justify the termination must be legal, and your termination under that provision must be reasonable.

For example, although an employer rules and regulations provision prohibiting stealing is unquestionably legal, whether you can fire a

---

[112] http://www.chinalawblog.com/2016/04/china-employer-rules-and-regulations-and-why-you-must-have-one.html

pregnant (or non-pregnant) employee for stealing things from your company can be tricky. Chinese courts used to uphold employers' decisions to let an employee go when the amount of the theft was really low. But over the years, we have seen a shift in court decisions that put more focus on the reasonableness of the employer's termination decision. So if your action is not proportionate to the infraction, the chances of it being upheld by a Chinese court are not high. For example, we would counsel our clients **not to** terminate an employee for stealing ten dollars' worth of office supplies.

It is also against the law to have an employee who is more than seven months pregnant, or who is nursing, work overtime or take night shifts. If your pregnant employee misses a half-day of work to go to her pregnancy checkup, it is not considered an absence of work under Chinese employment laws. So if you have her work late that day to make up the lost time, it's likely it will be considered working beyond normal hours, and that's overtime. If your pregnant employee submits a document from a health institution saying that her health no longer permits her to perform her usual job duties, you cannot demote her; you instead need to adjust her workload or her job duties to suit her existing situation. Generally speaking, you cannot as an employer dictate that you will recognize only certain doctors' notes from only certain hospitals. So again, be careful with what you put in your employer rules and regulations.[113]

You must also provide at least one hour per day during normal working hours for employees who breastfeed their babies and you must do this until the baby is a year old.

China amended its Law on Population and Family Planning, making it official that couples are encouraged to have two kids. The table below provides some basic information on the new maternity/paternity leave regulations in Beijing, Shanghai, and Guangdong:

	MATERNITY LEAVE	PATERNITY LEAVE
Beijing	128 days + 1-3	15 days

---

[113] http://www.chinalawblog.com/2016/09/china-employee-discipline-your-rules-and-regulations-are-just-a-starting-point.html

	months	
Shanghai	128 days	10 days
Guangdong	178 days	15 days

As is true of just about everything related to China's labor laws, its laws on pregnant and nursing employees are complicated and local.[114] And as is true of most of China's labor laws they get even more complicated when it comes to expats, where the local rules and practices are even more likely to be at odds with the national guidance.

Bottom Line: pregnant and nursing employees in China have all sorts of particularized rights. So as a China employer, you should be doubly careful in terminating a pregnant or nursing employee or even in changing their job schedule or duties. You should know both the national and the local rules and talk with your local labor authorities before making pretty much any move.

---

[114] http://www.chinalawblog.com/2015/12/china-employment-law-local-and-not-so-simple.html

HOW DO YOU HANDLE MATERNITY LEAVE IN BEIJING? IT'S LOCAL AND IT'S COMPLICATED

In China's Two Children Policy: What China Employers Should Know,[115] I wrote about how Beijing was in the process of amending its population and family regulations in response to the amended National Law on the same topic. For how China's employment laws are **both** national and local, check out China Employment Law: Local and Not So Simple.[116] Beijing has come out with its amendments and this post discusses their most salient points for Beijing employers.

Under its amended regulations, Beijing now requires a minimum of 128 days maternity leave (this is 30 days longer than the statutory minimum before the amendment). The special leave for a spouse whose wife gives birth is now 15 days (eight days longer than before). This is the same as in Guangdong Province[117] but five days longer than

---

[115] http://www.chinalawblog.com/2016/01/chinas-two-children-policy-what-china-employers-should-know.html

[116] http://www.chinalawblog.com/2015/12/china-employment-law-local-and-not-so-simple.html

[117] http://www.chinalawblog.com/2016/10/chinas-two-children-policy-a-quick-update.html

in Shanghai. The new regulations delete the special leave provision for late childbirth.

Beijing's new maternity and family leave regulations also provide that upon the female worker's request *and* the employer's consent, the maternity leave can be extended for another one to three months. This makes it possible for a female employee in Beijing to get up to 7.25 months of *paid* leave for childbirth, regardless of whether it is her first or second child. Under a strict interpretation of the Beijing maternity leave amendments, however, if the employer does not give its consent, the female worker cannot unilaterally make her leave longer than 128 days, or about 4.25 months.

However, as is typical of so many China employment laws and regulations, the rules on extending maternity leave are less than clear. In particular, it is not clear whether Beijing employers are free to say "no" to *all* employees seeking to extend their maternity leave or whether they must grant maternity leave extensions to employees with "good reasons" for not being able to return to work after the standard 128-day maternity leave. Given Beijing's longstanding pro-employee approach, our China employment lawyers are instructing our Beijing clients to have us review all the relevant facts relating to the employee's request for extended maternity leave and, most important, check with the local labor authorities before saying no. And do not forget that just like everywhere else in China, Beijing employers are generally prohibited from terminating an employee during his or her paternity/maternity leave, or to reduce that employee's wages in any way.

CHINA EMPLOYEE TERMINATION: AVOID THESE MISTAKES

I'm not entirely sure what is happening, but it feels as if about half my China labor law matters these days involve botched employee terminations. Terminating a China employee is never easy, but the following fairly easily remedied mistakes by China employers just keep showing up.

FAILING TO PAY STATUTORY SEVERANCE:

China employers far too often assume they do not need to pay their terminated employee any severance, [118] especially when the termination happens at the end date of a fixed-term employment contract. Many think that if their employment contracts are silent about severance, they need not pay. The mindset that an employment contract is an agreement made by two completely equal parties does not work for China. Whether you owe statutory severance depends not so much on your contracts, but on the rules in your locale *and* on the circumstances of the termination. For example, if the employee wishes to renew his or her contract, and the employer refuses, the employer is usually required to pay statutory severance. If the

---

[118] http://www.chinalawblog.com/2016/05/china-employment-law-statutory-severance.html

employer wants to renew on terms not as good as the employee's previous terms, and the employee refuses the renewal, the employer is usually required to pay statutory severance. These are just general rules. Some places (Beijing being one) require the employer to notify the employee in writing 30 days before the expiration of the current contract of its intent to end or renew the employment contract or pay in lieu of notice.

FAILING TO GET YOUR TERMINATED EMPLOYEE TO SIGN AN APPROPRIATE SETTLEMENT AND RELEASE AGREEMENT:

Think there is no need to enter into a termination/settlement agreement because your employee resigned[119] (and thus no statutory severance is owed)? It is true that the employee quit, but what made her do so? Did she leave for a better job or because you failed in some way to comply with Chinese labor laws and felt compelled to leave? If it's the latter, and if you don't address the issues via a settlement, you could end up having to answer in front of a judge or an arbitrator. If your employee's departure has nothing to do with your wrongdoing, you should document that, and even then, you may want a signed agreement that releases you from any future claims. I cannot tell you how many times we have seen instances where an employer would have saved big money by paying an "unnecessary" severance to avoid the completely "unexpected" and costly litigation that followed.

FAILING TO FORMALLY EXECUTE KEY EMPLOYMENT DOCUMENTS

As a China employer you should have most of your employee-related documents formally chopped. Your legal representative's signature alone is not enough. Your legal representative's signature and your company chop is not enough if the employee's signature is not there. Along the same lines, your employee agreements should specify the date of execution. If the document is long, it may be a good idea to fan out the pages and stamp your company chop across all the pages. Better yet — have your employee sign his or her name across all the pages.

---

[119] http://www.chinalawblog.com/2016/08/when-your-china-employees-leaves.html

BOTTOM LINE: I know this sounds harsh, but you should plan for your employee terminations pretty much the day you hire.

What are the ABCs of China's New Work Permit System for Foreigners?

China recently initiated a *pilot* program for foreigner work permits that integrates foreigner entry employment licenses and foreign expert employment licenses into one "foreigner employment permit." The PRC State Administration of Foreign Experts Affairs (SAFEA) has been tasked with carrying out this new program. This pilot program is intended to streamline current application and administration procedures and processes and to attract more high level foreign talent to China. SAFEA has implemented this pilot program in a few cities and provinces, including Beijing, Tianjin, Hebei, Shanghai, Anhui, Shandong, Guangdong, Sichuan, and Ningxia. As of April 1, 2017, the program has gone national.

Here are a few highlights of this pilot program:

Most important, the current foreign expert work license and foreigner employment license will be integrated into one document called the foreigner work license notice. The employer and foreign applicant will be able to complete and submit the license form electronically. The original "alien employment permit" and "foreign expert certificate" will be integrated into one permit called the foreigner work permit. Every foreigner will have one permit number per foreigner work permit, which will be used by the same individual for life. Effective April 1, 2017, the foreigner work license notice (外国人工作许可通知) and foreigner work permit (外国人工作许可证) are being formally used. The currently effective employment licenses can continue to be used up to their respective expiration dates.

China recently enacted a nationwide administration service system for foreigners coming to China. The application materials required for submission are much less than before, and application letters, expert/employment permit application forms, bilingual resumes, and letters of intent for employment will be eliminated, reducing the documentation foreigners will need to submit by half.

Foreigners are divided into three categories: (A) high-level talent; (B) professional personnel; and (C) foreigners who are nontechnical or service workers hired on a temporary/seasonal basis. A score system considers various criteria for each foreign applicant, such as salary, educational background, experience, and length of service. The goal is to encourage foreigners in the first category (A levels), exert control over foreigners in the second category (B levels), and strictly restrict foreigners in the last category (C levels).

A "green channel" also is now available to a high-level foreign talent. These high-level foreigners no longer need submit any hard copies of the documents required to apply for a foreigner work permit notice or for a visa application before entering China and the review and approval period for these foreigners is considerably shorter than for foreigners at the other two levels.

How will all of this play out in practice? We shall see and we shall keep you posted on our China Employment Law blog.[120]

---

[120] http://www.chinalawblog.com

WHAT'S GOING ON WITH CHINA'S TWO CHILDREN POLICY? A QUICK UPDATE

As promised,[121] here is a follow-up on what's happening in Guangdong. Pursuant to the amended PRC Law on Population and Family Planning and China's nationwide two-children policy, major provinces/cities in China have all extended the mandatory maternity leave. As with almost everything having to do with Chinese employment laws, there is a variance in such rules around the nation. See China Employment Law: Local and Not So Simple.[122]

As I previously wrote,[123] Guangdong was the first province in China to come up with its own amended regulations for dealing with two child families, which took effect on January 1, 2016. This amendment increased maternity leave from 98 to 128 days. Now these regulations have been amended again, extending the maternity leave to 178 days, 50 days more than other major cities such as Shanghai (128 days). The

[121] http://www.chinalawblog.com/2016/01/chinas-two-children-policy-what-china-employers-should-know.html

[122] http://www.chinalawblog.com/2015/12/china-employment-law-local-and-not-so-simple.html

[123] http://www.chinalawblog.com/2016/01/chinas-two-children-policy-what-china-employers-should-know.html

special leave for a spouse whose wife gives birth stays the same at 15 days, which puts it roughly in the middle of the chart as compared to other places: for example, it is longer than Shanghai (10 days) but shorter than Guangxi (25 days).

If you think this leave time is long, check out the leave time in Heilongjiang or Gansu: both require that employers give their female workers 180 days of maternity leave. One question our China lawyers often get is how/whether this applies to all employees, including expats. The spirit of the national law seems to indicate yes, but this is anything but a simple question. To get a definitive answer, you should check what your own employer/employee documents say **and** the rules in your specific locale. On top of this, because these sorts of things can be highly fact-specific and you do not want to get anything wrong, it is important that your own employee contracts be clear and in compliance with all applicable laws.

DIY China Employment Law: Really?

Chinese employment law is governed by an almost overwhelming number of laws, regulations, measures, policies, circulars, meeting minutes, and other dictums. The rules may be national, regional, provincial, city-wide, or just district-wide within a particular city. Many are unwritten and can only be known by direct communication with the local labor bureau.

The increased availability of translated PRC laws has, in some ways, made the problem worse, because — even assuming the law is still valid and the translation is accurate — a single law, standing alone, paints an incomplete picture and often implies a course of action that is just plain wrong. Some of the worst-positioned employment cases we get are where the client has made key decisions based on their understanding of a single translated law. Far too often these decisions directly contravene local rules, which are rarely translated and often unknown to anyone not doing employment work. In China, the local rules can be highly differentiated. A policy that works fine in one city could get your company into hot water in another. For example: non-compete agreements that do not specify the amount of compensation are likely enforceable in Shanghai but not in Guangdong.

A friend of mine works as the in-house employment lawyer for a massive technology company in China, and he admitted to me that he frequently wakes up in the middle of the night to double-check his work. He has to deal with so many cities in China, and he is constantly worried that he may have missed something. I empathize with him; there are so many rules, and they change so often. And even if you find the applicable rules, you still need to analyze how they apply to the specific situation. I am on the phone nearly every day with local labor law agencies across China, asking questions about their interpretation of a given law/regulation/rule/etc. Anyone who knows China knows that if a rule clearly appears to say one thing but the local authorities believe it says something else, your reliance on the clear meaning will be for naught.

As with most things, the trick is knowing when you need a lawyer and when you don't. For more on this, check out Inexpensive China Lawyers. Really?[124]

---

[124] http://www.chinalawblog.com/2015/05/inexpensive-china-lawyers-really.html

CHINA EMPLOYMENT LAWS AND LIFETIME EMPLOYMENT

It is important to select an appropriate initial fixed employment term because in most places in China employees are automatically converted into "open contract" employees when the fixed term concludes. An open-term labor contract means the employer must (with very few exceptions) retain the employee until his or her retirement age.

China's labor law provides that an employee is entitled to an open-term contract under the following circumstances:

1. The employee has been continuously working for the employer for ten years.
2. The employer is implementing the labor contract system for the first time, or the employer is a state-owned enterprise and went through reorganization and executes a labor contract with the employee, and the employee has been continuously working for the employer for 10 years and is less than 10 years from his or her legal retirement age.

3. After execution of two consecutive fixed-term labor contracts (unless grounds for termination exists).

The PRC Labor Contract Law is very pro-employee when it comes to conversions to an open-term labor contract. At renewal or execution of the labor contract, *unless* the employee requests a fixed-term labor contract, an open-term labor contract shall be concluded. And many Chinese courts (especially outside Shanghai) strictly read this language and nearly always find that an open-term labor contract has been created.

For example, in a Jiangsu Province case, after executing two consecutive fixed-term contracts, the employer and the employee entered into a third fixed-term contract, at the end of which the employer chose not to extend the contract. The employee sued and the court held that the employer bore the burden of producing evidence proving the employee had been the one to request the third fixed-term labor contract. Lacking conclusive proof of this, the court held that the employer had failed to meet its burden of proof and its decision to execute the third fixed-term labor contract was wrongful. Because the employer's decision to end the employment relationship upon expiration of the third fixed-term contract was illegal, the employee was entitled to be converted to a lifetime employee and the employer was ordered to pay the employee **double** the employee's monthly wage from the time an open-term contract should have been entered.

Oh, and don't forget that you could be deemed to have entered into an open-term employment contract with your employee if the employee works for you for more than a year without having a written employment contract.

BOTTOM LINE: make sure your employment contracts are current[125] and you are using the right term of employment.

---

[125] http://www.chinalawblog.com/2015/05/china-employment-contracts-if-yours-are-not-current-you-have-a-problem.html

CHINA EMPLOYER YEAR-END REVIEW? CHECK THESE NINE THINGS OFF YOUR LIST

Whenever the end of the year approaches and our clients contact us to help them conduct their various year-end reviews/audits, one of the most important things we do is the employer-employee audit. The following are some of the basic things you should have on your employer-employee review list:

1. **Employment contracts.** Do you have a written contract[126] with every single one of your employees, including part-time employees? Are all your employment contracts current?

2. **Employer rules and regulations (aka employee handbook).** Do you have a set of rules and regulations?[127] More important, does what you have work for China? Has it been made available to all your employees? Have your employees signed a receipt proving they actually received it?

---

[126] http://www.chinalawblog.com/2016/04/china-employment-contracts-ten-things-to-consider.html

[127] http://www.chinalawblog.com/2016/09/china-employee-discipline-your-rules-and-regulations-are-just-a-starting-point.html

3. **Dispatched employees.** Are you in compliance with the labor dispatch laws?[128] Do you have more dispatched workers than the statutory maximum? Are you using dispatched workers for positions that should be filled by a regular employee? Are you using dispatched workers when you could directly hire them as your own employees?

4. **Female employees, especially those who are pregnant or nursing.** Are you providing the labor protections and conditions required under relevant laws? Are you providing maternity leave in accordance with the law?

5. **Working time, rest, and vacation days.** Have you made arrangements so your employees can take their vacation days?[129] Are you making sure your employees who are designated to work under the standard working hours system do not exceed their standard working time? Are you making sure that whenever it is necessary to incur overtime,[130] the employees follow your internal procedure and that you pay the employees for their overtime? Are you current on the alternate working hours system renewal? Are you giving your employees on these systems enough rest and due consideration to their health?

6. **Employee compensation.** Are you meeting the minimum wage requirements? Note that several provinces and cities, including Shanghai, Jiangsu, and Chongqing recently raised their minimum wage standards. Are you paying your employees on time? When you withhold payment from an employee, do you explain the reasons to the employee and document the situation so you will be able to show your action was reasonable and lawful?

7. **Social insurance contributions.** Are you making all mandatory social insurance contributions? In places where

---

[128] http://www.chinalawblog.com/2016/07/china-labor-dispatch-rules-why-did-you-ever-think-it-would-be-easy.html

[129] http://www.chinalawblog.com/2016/02/china-employee-vacation-law.html

[130] http://www.chinalawblog.com/2012/02/overtime_pay_in_china_what_ya_gonna_do.html

employers are required to make contributions for expats,[131] are you paying into the expats' social insurance accounts or have you otherwise made arrangements in the employee's contract (*provided* it's permissible in your locale)? The good news is that China is going to modify the base for social insurance contributions, which will ease the burden on employers. The bad news is that many of the companies we review are not in compliance with applicable rules on this.

8. **Employee non-competes.** Do you have signed employee non-competes[132] from all of your employees who might harm you by competing with you? What about non-solicitation agreements?

9. **Employee terminations.** Are you handling all of your employee terminations[133] according to law? Do you document your employee terminations? Do you timely transfer your terminated employees' files and social insurance accounts?

BOTTOM LINE: if you are not in compliance with the Chinese labor laws, get in compliance as soon as you can. China is only getting tougher on employer violations.[134]

---

[131] http://www.chinalawblog.com/2016/08/hiring-foreign-employees-in-china.html

[132] http://www.chinalawblog.com/2016/10/china-employee-non-competes-the-who-what-when-where-and-how-much.html

[133] http://www.chinalawblog.com/2016/10/china-employee-termination-avoid-these-mistakes.html

[134] http://www.chinalawblog.com/2016/10/chinas-employment-laws-get-them-right-or-face-very-public-consequences.html

WHAT DO YOU NEED TO KNOW ABOUT CHINA EMPLOYEE TERMINATIONS AND THE NEW TWO CHILD POLICY?

In China's new two-child era, couples are allowed (even encouraged) to have two kids, but no more, unless an exception applies.

Can an employer in China unilaterally terminate an employee who is having more than two kids or otherwise violates the relevant laws on family planning and population control? This is an easy question to answer regarding employees of state-owned enterprises and government agencies. Employees at such organizations are subject to more stringent regulations because they are government employees and they can be unilaterally terminated for having more than two children (still, the legality will depend on the *local* regulations).

The question that most concerns China employment lawyers and China employers alike is what can privately owned companies do in this situation. As I have said many times and will say again: as is so often the case when it comes to China employment law, the answer(s) is localized and complicated.[135] For example, Shenzhen generally

---

[135] http://www.chinalawblog.com/2015/12/china-employment-law-local-and-not-so-simple.html

prohibits employers from unilaterally terminating an employee for violating family planning laws, but it also gives its employers some leeway by allowing them to deal with this issue in their employment contracts, collective contracts, and/or their employer rules and regulations.[136] But because my statement regarding the rules in Shenzhen is based on seminar minutes from a Shenzhen Human Resources and Social Security Bureau meeting, the legal authority for even this in Shenzhen is somewhat unclear.

It is also important for any employer in China to understand that because female employees are a special class for whom Chinese laws provide extra protections, unilaterally terminating a pregnant employee is almost always going to be more difficult and problematic than it may first appear under the written laws and regulations. For this reason, when our employer-clients seek our counsel on unilaterally terminating a pregnant employee we nearly always seek out alternatives, including a mutual termination with an appropriate Chinese language settlement agreement. See China Employee Termination: Avoid These Mistakes.[137]

A related question is whether an employer can put in its rules and regulations that violating relevant family planning laws warrants employee termination. As noted above, such a provision may hold water in Shenzhen, but not necessarily elsewhere in China. Many cities in China are of the view that because the employee who has violated China's family planning laws will be, or is already, facing fines imposed by the authorities overseeing family planning and population, it would be too harsh *to also* allow the employee to be unilaterally terminated for the same thing, no matter what is in the employer's rules and regulations and no matter how "flawless" the termination. Beijing used to split on this question, with some of its labor bureaus holding that employers may rely on their rules and regulations to fire an employee for violating China's family planning laws, while others held the opposite position. Around the time of International Women's Day in 2015, Beijing's Second Intermediate Court made its position clear in a press conference: employers cannot unilaterally terminate employees

---

[136] http://www.chinalawblog.com/2016/04/china-employer-rules-and-regulations-and-why-you-must-have-one.html

[137] http://www.chinalawblog.com/2016/10/china-employee-termination-avoid-these-mistakes.html

for violating China's family planning laws. An employer may discipline such an employee (but not terminate him or her), **_provided_** there is an applicable provision in the employee rules and regulations. In other words, if you have no such rules in place, you do not even get to discipline the employee. However, whether this Court pronouncement settles the issue even for Beijing is still unclear.

If an employee violates China's family planning laws, can the employer refuse to provide the extra protections normally provided employees during pregnancy, such as no overtime or an adjustment of workload?

As is nearly always the case with any China labor law issues, the answer varies by locale, but generally speaking, a pregnant/nursing employee who violates China's family planning laws should be treated the same as other pregnant/nursing employees while on the job. However, other benefits after childbirth, such as paid maternity leave, can generally be withheld from an employee who has violated the family planning laws, though this too varies by location.

I should emphasize how important it is not to try to remove an employee's legal protections by having them sign a contract that purports to do so. A fairly recent case out of Shanghai (a fairly employer-friendly city) makes this clear.

In this case, an employee entered into an employment contract with her employer on her first day, March 1. This employee was required to fill out an employee form before she officially started. As she was not married at that time, she checked the box for "single" on the form. The contract expressly provided that if any information provided by the employee was untrue, the employer would have the right to void the contract and unilaterally terminate the employee. The employer's handbook contained similar provisions and also required its employees to update the employer within 10 days if any personal information, such as marital status, had changed. The employee became pregnant a few days after her first day and started going to checkups but she never informed her employer about her pregnancy until October.

The employee married in May and her employer approved her marriage leave. A couple of months before her expected due date, the employee provided her employer with a doctor's note saying she would need to go on maternity leave because she would need to rest before her scheduled C-section. The employee requested paid maternity leave, but her employer immediately terminated her because she had "deceived" them by not providing accurate information about her personal situation. The employer then brought a labor arbitration claim against the employee seeking to declare her employment contract void. The employee filed counterclaims demanding her salary during her sick leave and maternity leave, as well as double statutory severance for unlawful termination and reinstatement of her position.

The employer lost on most of the claims and was ordered to pay the employee her salary during her sick days and during her maternity leave, and also to pay for her social insurance until the last day of her extended maternity leave. The court acknowledged that the employee should have updated her employer on her marital/pregnancy status sooner, but nothing she had done justified her unilateral termination. The labor arbitration committee did not discuss the employee's claim for double statutory severance for unlawful termination. And because the employee withdrew her claim for reinstatement of her position, and did not argue for unlawful termination severance at the court level, the court did not discuss those claims either.

The court stated in the first sentence of its decision that "employees' legal interests are protected by law" and female workers "giving birth is a natural and legal right and must be accorded full protection." Although this case was decided before China's new two-child policy, and although some of the legal aspects of this case have changed, what has not changed is that it is simply not possible to remove most worker protections via contract. Most important, as a China employer, you should know and follow *all* the relevant laws and regulations and rules (national, regional, and local down to your specific district within your city) before terminating or even penalizing one of your employees.

WHAT EIGHT THINGS CAN YOU DO TO IMPROVE YOUR RULES AND REGULATIONS?

Whenever the end of the year approaches, regardless of whether you conduct a year-end employer-employee audit,[138] update and refine your China employee rules and regulations.[139] As this is usually (and should be) a much longer document than your employee contracts, doing this will probably take a fair amount of work. To make this task just a little bit easier, I suggest you focus on the following eight basic things to do to whip your China employee rules and regulations into shape for the new year:

1. Make sure the Chinese version of your document is in tip-top shape. Far too many companies have a non-lawyer translate their rules and regulations into Chinese and far too many companies therefore have Chinese language rules and regulations that are not appropriately written for a court or other tribunal. Make sure this is not the case for yours, and while you are doing so, check it for typos, etc. You should also

---

[138] http://www.chinalawblog.com/2016/11/china-employer-year-end-review-check-these-nine-things-off-your-list.html

[139] http://www.chinalawblog.com/2016/04/china-employer-rules-and-regulations-and-why-you-must-have-one.html

make sure that your Chinese version lines up with your English version. For example, if your English version says "do not" and your Chinese says "do," you know there is something wrong (I see this sort of basic error all the time when conducting employer-employee audits).

2. If your company's rules and regulations are in Chinese only, you really should have an English translation done. You as the employer will need to refer to this document when you make most employee decisions and unless all your employees who will be making these decisions are fluent in written Chinese, you need a well-written version in English as well.

3. Focus first on the sections of your rules and regulations that matter most to managing your China employees. This means you can, for the most part, gloss over any mission statement. Focus instead on sections where any failure to follow what is written will get you into big trouble. When I am asked by a company to review their rules and regulations to let them know if it will work for China, the first thing I look at is the section on disciplinary actions[140] because that section is so often litigated. If that section is not well crafted, I immediately know that revising the rules and regulations is in order.

4. If there is a section of your rules and regulations on which your employees are frequently commenting, questioning, or voicing their concerns, this is a section you should be reviewing and probably revising.

5. If you are seeing employee infractions that are not well addressed or addressed at all in your rules and regulations, put something in there for those, or fix what is already there. Do this before one of your employees commits this infraction and you find yourself (again) in a situation where you are powerless to do something about it.

6. Make sure you use the appropriate word/phrase in your rules and regulations to actually accomplish what you are seeking to accomplish. If you want to impose an obligation on your employees, make sure you use the word "must" and as noted above, and make sure the Chinese version also says "must."

---

[140] http://www.chinalawblog.com/2016/09/china-employee-discipline-your-rules-and-regulations-are-just-a-starting-point.html

Saying "employees are expected to do something" does not usually cut it, and yet our China employment lawyers see language like this in rules and regulations all the time. If all you want to do is encourage your employees to do something, fine, but your rules and regulations are almost never the best (or even the right) place to do that. The rules and regulations are called rules and regulations for a reason; they should be used to clearly delineate what your employees *must* do and *must not* do *and* make clear the repercussions for violations. If your rules and regulations say "DO NOT DO XXX!!!", and then do not make clear that doing XXX will lead to termination, you likely cannot legally terminate an employee who does XXX no matter how large the font or how many exclamation points you use.

7. Remove from your rules and regulations anything that no longer complies with China's ever shifting labor laws. And when I say China labor laws, I mean any applicable national, regional, or local law. See China Employment Law: Local and Not So Simple.[141] Just by way of one very common example: if your rules and regulations provide for termination for an infraction that is not a terminable offense where your employees are located, there is a good chance you will engage in ineffective terminations that waste your company a lot of time and money by creating unnecessary employee-employer disputes.

8. Make sure your rules and regulations *clearly* spell out incentives, bonuses and benefits. And if your rules and regulations say that you will be providing any of these, you really should provide them. Well over half the rules and regulations we review or audit need substantial cleaning up of these provisions, and a good portion of the China labor law disputes on which our China labor lawyers are retained involve these sections.

Bottom line: if you have employees in China, resolve to clean up and improve your employee rules and regulations by the New Year.

---

[141] http://www.chinalawblog.com/2015/12/china-employment-law-local-and-not-so-simple.html

WHAT ARE SIX MYTHS ABOUT WORKING HOURS AND OVERTIME?

Working hours for most China employees are usually determined under China's "standard working hours system," and in most places in China, that means a 40-hour work week — eight hours a day and five days a week. This system does not allow for a lot of flexibility because work done outside the normal working hours is considered overtime that obligates the employer to pay overtime. I am finding that foreign employers are often (virtually always, actually) confused about China's working hours and they often believe (and repeat to me) the following six myths regarding working hours and overtime in China, all of which are daily costing foreign companies extra money in China.

Myth 1: China's overtime rules are similar to the exempt employee rules in the United States.

Wrong. For example, it does *not* matter how much your China employee gets paid. Your China employee might be making three times the average salary in the city where you are located (this amount is a common threshold for a number of things under Chinese employment law). Generally speaking, you must pay *all* overtime.

Myth 2: Managerial employees are exempt from overtime pay.

If a manager works under the standard working hours system, overtime incurred must be paid. If your manager(s) have been approved to work under an alternate working hours system[142] (usually the flexible working hours system) you can avoid paying overtime on most occasions, except for (and this depends on the locale!) time worked on a legal holiday such as New Year's Day, Chinese New Year, National Day, etc.

Myth 3: An employer and employee can contractually agree to have the employee work under alternate working hours.

Nope.

Most places in China require **prior** government approval for an employee to work under a non-standard working hours system. The employee's written consent alone is usually not sufficient.

Myth 4: Comp time can negate overtime obligations.

Not necessarily. This depends on the employee's situation and the locale in China. If an employee working under the standard working hours system stays beyond the normal eight hour work day, you must pay overtime, which is usually 150% of that employee's normal wage. But in most locales in China, an employee who works during a weekend can be compensated with comp time. However, if you are unable to give the employee comp time (perhaps because you mistakenly failed to do so or because you simply were too busy), most locales in China will require you pay 200% of the employee's normal wage, or 300% if the work was on a legal holiday.

Myth 5: An employee on an alternate working hours system[143] need never be paid overtime.

Be careful. Again, this — like pretty much everything else employment related in China — depends largely on the locale.[144] Most places in

---

[142] http://www.chinalawblog.com/2014/06/china-2.html

[143] http://www.chinalawblog.com/2014/06/chinas-forty-hour-work-week-is-mandatory-except-when-its-not-part-ii.html

China require the employer pay even alternate hour employees overtime for time worked during a Chinese legal holiday. Also, we cannot count the number of times a foreign employee has insisted that such and such employee is under the alternate working hours system and one of our China labor lawyers has discovered that was never the case or is no longer the case due to a failure to timely renew.

Myth 6: The employee (not the employer) is required to keep track of time for overtime pay.

Tell this to the many foreign employers who thought this was the case and then ended up having to pay all sorts of back overtime pay when the employee left to avoid getting sued for not having done so. You as the employer need to document your employees' overtime. And just because an employee has not yet hit you up for it, it does *not* mean you don't owe it. Your rules and regulations[145] should contain a section setting out your company's overtime policy, including the internal procedures that your employees must follow for securing approval before incurring overtime, and your procedures for reporting such overtime.

BOTTOM LINE: make sure you understand the national, regional, and local laws that apply to overtime in the city where you are located.

---

[144] http://www.chinalawblog.com/2015/12/china-employment-law-local-and-not-so-simple.html

[145] http://www.chinalawblog.com/2016/04/china-employer-rules-and-regulations-and-why-you-must-have-one.html

CHINA'S CYBERSECURITY LAW AND EMPLOYEE PERSONAL INFORMATION

The PRC government promulgated its Cybersecurity Law on November 7, 2016, with an effective date of June 1, 2017. To say that foreign tech firms are concerned about the impact of this new law on their business in China would be an understatement. In addition to tech firms, our China lawyers have received a steady stream of questions from clients with China WFOEs who are concerned about an entirely different set of issues. Article 35 of the law states that "personal information and other important data gathered or produced by critical information infrastructure network operators during operations within the mainland territory of the People's Republic of China, shall store it within mainland China." Our clients keep asking what this will mean for them.

The surprising answer is not much.

Any company that operates a WFOE in China collects personal information about its employees. China's new cybersecurity law defines personal information as "all kinds of information, recorded electronically or through other means, that taken alone or together with other information, is sufficient to identify a natural person's identity, including, but not limited to, natural persons' full names, birth dates, identification numbers, personal biometric information, addresses, telephone numbers, and so forth." Certainly, the standard information any company maintains on its employees will qualify as personal information under China's new cybersecurity law.

In the EU and various other jurisdictions, such personal information must be maintained *within* the jurisdiction and there should be no transfer of such information across borders. This causes many problems for companies that seek to manage an international workforce through a central location.

So what clients keep asking our China attorneys is whether China's new cybersecurity laws will establish the same sort of protective system *within* China. The simple answer is that it will not. China does not have a comprehensive law or regulations relating to the collection, processing, or transfer of employee data gathered by a WFOE or other business entity in the normal course of its China business operations. And China's new cybersecurity law does *not* change that situation.

The cybersecurity law specifically provides that the personal data maintenance and collection rules apply only to *critical infrastructure network operators.* Network operator is defined as "network owners, managers and network service providers." In more general terms, this means telecom operators and Internet ISPs. The requirements do *not* apply to the China business operations of normal private businesses with respect to their normal record keeping requirements for their employees.

Even though nothing has legally changed in China, it is still best practice for foreign employers in China to follow the basic rules the PRC government imposes more generally in the consumer context on the collection and maintenance of personal information, including the following:

1. Be sure the disclosing party (your employee) is aware that the company maintains personal information. The company should have a written policy (in Chinese and in English) on how long that information is maintained and that policy should be revealed to the employee.

2. You should not collect more personal information than necessary.

3. You should maintain the confidentiality of the personal information you collect and maintain. That means you should limit internal access to that information and you should take

proper security measures to prevent a data breach of the company's online systems.

4. You should not sell or otherwise transfer the personal information to any third party. Stated more bluntly, do not sell employee personal information to marketers or spammers.

CONCLUSION

Life is really simple, but men insist on making it complicated.

~ Confucius

We have covered a tremendous amount of detail in this reference guide to China employment law. We hope we have given you and your team useful insights into what to do (and what not to do) to get the results your company needs – and to avoid trouble.

We started our tour by diving deep into contracts. We touched on best practices, common mistakes, and scenarios that occur with some frequency, especially for foreign companies that set up shop in China.

Next, we explored key challenges China employers face. How should you handle pregnant and nursing employees, for example? How does Chinese law handle mass layoffs? What are the consequences of the fact that locality is so important to China labor law? How can you keep up with the essentials of labor law without running yourself ragged or getting distracted from your key business and competencies?

Finally, we answered questions that many of our clients (and blog readers) have had about how China employment law works in the crucible of the real world and gave you links to go deeper into topics that are pressing and/or interesting to you.

We hope you enjoyed this guide and got value from it. We're also standing by to help you address your China employment issues and to help give you the clarity and peace of mind you need to make smarter, more profitable employer decisions. You can get in touch with me at 1-206-224-5657 or grace@harrisbricken.com or learn more about us at

http://harrisbricken.com

ABOUT THE AUTHOR

Grace Yang is an attorney with Harris Bricken who focuses on international business and China law. She is a member of the Washington State Bar Association, New York State Bar Association, Asian Bar Association of Washington, and King County Bar Association.

Grace received her B.A. degree in Law from Peking University and her J.D. degree from University of Washington School of Law. Grace is the lead China employment law attorney at Harris Bricken and she frequently contributes to the China Law Blog with posts on China employment law.

Grace has many years of experience providing China employment law counsel to both China employers and employees in various industries.

GET SPECIAL DEALS ON MORE BEST SELLING BOOKS

Get discounts and special deals on our best selling books at

www.tckpublishing.com/bookdeals

www.ingramcontent.com/pod-product-compliance
Lightning Source LLC
Chambersburg PA
CBHW060527210326
41519CB00014B/3147